Systemic Group Therapy

A TRIADIC MODEL

D1491263

TITLES OF RELATED INTEREST

Corey, Marianne Schneider, and Corey, Gerald, *Groups: Process and Practice*, Fifth Edition

Corey, Gerald, *Theory and Practice of Group Counseling*, Fourth Edition

Corey, Gerald, *Student Manual for Theory and Practice of Group Counseling*, Fourth Edition

Corey, Gerald, Corey, Marianne Schneider, Callanan, Patrick, and Russell, J. Michael, *Group Techniques*, Second Edition

Donigian, Jeremiah, and Malnati, Richard, *Critical Incidents in Group Therapy*

Egan, Gerald, *Face to Face: The Small-Group Experience and Interpersonal Growth*

Egan, Gerald, *Interpersonal Living: A Skills/Contract Approach to Human-Relations Training in Groups*

Forsyth, Donelson R., *Group Dynamics*, Second Edition

Jacobs, Edward E., Harvill, Riley L., and Masson, Robert L., *Group Counseling: Strategies and Skills*, Second Edition

Kottler, Jeffrey A., *Advanced Group Leadership*

Yalom, Irvin D., *Understanding Group Psychotherapy: Process and Practice* (Video). *Volume I: Outpatients; Volume II: Inpatients; Volume III: An Interview*

SYSTEMIC GROUP THERAPY

A TRIADIC MODEL

Jeremiah Donigian
*State University of New York
College at Brockport*

Richard Malnati

Brooks/Cole Publishing Company

I(T)P®An International Thomson Publishing Company

Pacific Grove • Albany • Belmont • Bonn • Boston • Cincinnati • Detroit • Johannesburg • London
Madrid • Melbourne • Mexico City • New York • Paris • Singapore • Tokyo • Toronto • Washington

 A CLAIREMONT BOOK

Sponsoring Editor: *Eileen Murphy*
Marketing Team: *Jean Thompson,*
Romy Taormina
Editorial Assistant: *Lisa Blanton*
Production Editor: *Keith Faivre*

Manuscript Editor: *Carole Freddo*
Interior: *Kelly Shoemaker*
Cover Design: *Roger Knox*
Typesetting: *Joan Mueller Cochrane*
Printing and Binding: *Malloy Lithographing, Inc.*

For more information, contact:

BROOKS/COLE PUBLISHING COMPANY
511 Forest Lodge Road
Pacific Grove, CA 93950
USA

International Thomson Publishing Europe
Berkshire House 168–173
High Holborn
London WC1V 7AA
England

Thomas Nelson Australia
102 Dodds Street
South Melbourne, 3205
Victoria, Australia

Nelson Canada
1120 Birchmount Road
Scarborough, Ontario
Canada M1K 5G4

International Thomson Editores
Seneca 53
Col. Polanco
11560 México D. F. México

International Thomson Publishing GmbH
Königswinterer Strasse 418
53227 Bonn
Germany

International Thomson Publishing Asia
221 Henderson Road
#05–10 Henderson Building
Singapore 0315

International Thomson Publishing Japan
Hirakawacho Kyowa Building, 3F
2-2-1 Hirakawacho
Chiyoda-ku, Tokyo 102
Japan

Printed in the United States of America

10   9   8   7   6   5   4   3   2   1

Library of Congress Cataloging-in-Publication Data

Donigian, Jeremiah, [date]
    Systemic group therapy : a triadic model / Jeremiah Donigian,
Richard Malnati.
        p.   cm.
    Includes bibliographical references and index.
    ISBN 0-534-34518-2 (alk. paper)
    1. Group counseling. 2. Group psychotherapy.   I. Malnati,
Richard J.   II. Title.
BF637.C6D614   1997
616.89'152--dc20   96-17211
                                                         CIP

To our parents
Elsie and Harry Donigian
Angelina and Roger Malnati

*Good leadership consists of doing less
and being more.*

—John Heider, *The Tao of Leadership*

PREFACE

We were midway through the writing of this book when I lost my co-leader, colleague, co-writer, and dear friend. Concluding the writing of it was symbolic of a number of things for me.

Dick Malnati was a teacher at heart. He was truly at home both in the classroom and in leading seminars on group therapy. When he conceived the idea of this book, he envisioned it as a useful addition to the course syllabi of those who teach group therapy. Now that Dick's vision has at last been realized, I find myself able to bring a peaceful closure to that chapter of my life in which my friend made such an important contribution. While we collaborated on every aspect of the book, I have tried to make certain that Dick's voice and seminal ideas are heard in these pages. (I hope I managed to do that, Dick.)

I would be remiss if I did not acknowledge the very significant help I received from Claire Verduin throughout a period when I needed support and understanding. A simple thank-you hardly seems adequate to express what her caring and encouragement have meant to me. I am truly grateful you were there, Claire.

To Eileen Murphy I wish to offer my heartfelt thanks. She had (for me) the unenviable position of assuming the reins after Claire Verduin retired. She managed to make the transition appear effortless and guided the manuscript through its final stages, ultimately to its publication. To Keith Faivre, Romy Taormina, Jennifer Petitt, Kelly Shoemaker, and the rest of the production team, you were all gracious and very helpful. Thank you.

I am grateful to the following reviewers whose helpful criticism improved this book: Virginia B. Allen, Idaho State University; Mary Ballou, Northeastern University; Richard B. Caple, University of Missouri—Columbia; Jack A. Duncan, Virginia Commonwealth University; R. Blair Olson, Henderson State University; Paula Helen Stanley, Radford University; Cilla Tragesser, Western Washington University; and Donald E. Ward, Pittsburg State University—Kansas.

I also extend my sincere thanks to the students who were with us as this book went through various stages of development and who offered many suggestions for improving it. Their feedback was invaluable.

Finally, I thank Dorothy Reed for her patience and tenacity in accommodating constant rewrites of the manuscript.

Jeremiah Donigian

INTRODUCTION

We undertook the writing of this book as part of our long-standing mission to "demystify" the phenomenon of group process (Donigian & Malnati, 1987). In conducting seminars and workshops on group therapy throughout the country, we have often been impressed by the hunger on the part of students and practitioners alike to acquire an understanding of *how* and *why* counseling and therapy groups work as they do.

We ask you to set aside your current perceptions of what group therapy is as you read this book so that you will be open to our views on group therapy. We know that some of *what* we have to say about group therapy will be familiar to you. However, we believe the way we *reframe the process* of group therapy will be new to you.

We begin Part I by setting group process within the context of General Systems Theory (GST).* Here we present the three subsystems—which we refer to as *elements*—that we have identified as making up therapy groups. These elements are critical to the argument of this text, for we take the position that group therapists need to consciously attend to them and to their patterns of interdependent interaction throughout the life of the groups they lead. This reframing of the group into three elements encourages group therapists

---

*We encourage those of you who want to acquire an in-depth understanding of GST and how it is related to group therapy to seek out Agazarian and Peters (1981), Agazarian and Janoffs (1993), Davidson (1983), Durkin (1981), Napier and Gershenfeld (1993), Nichols and Schwartz (1994), Vanderkolk (1985), and von Bertalanffy (1968).

to think of group process as a systemic interaction between the leader, the individual member, and the group. We strongly believe that group therapists need to be conscious of how the behaviors of any one element affect the other two. No event is to be considered in isolation of the three elements, for each element contributed in some way to the event's occurrence and each, in turn, is in some way affected by it.

Our focus throughout the book is on the patterned interaction among the three elements. In Part I, we explore the seven primary group processes that are released by the interaction of the three elements. We begin with Contagion and conclude with the Instillation of Hope.

Part II introduces a five-stage development model of group therapy. It also addresses the factors that influence each of the three elements. These are critical to understanding the way the member(s), the leader(s), and the group behave. Our intention is to help leaders learn to *listen for* these factors and to hear *what* they are communicating about the three elements. In so doing, leaders will grasp why the elements behave as they do. We have identified 15 factors that affect the elements. These include (six) Systems of Communication, History, Themes, Norms and Standards, Stages, Cohesion, Power versus Influence, and (three) Structural Factors.

Part III expands upon the five-stage development model introduced in Part II. Each of the stages is described according to the same format: characteristics that reflect the stage, the behaviors in which each of the elements engage, and sample process questions leaders may ask themselves regarding each of the elements. The sample questions are intended not only to help leaders avoid doing individual therapy but also to demystify the processes that are common to each element at each stage of the group's development.

We conclude by describing, in Part IV, the processes for conceptualizing and deciding which intervention to employ. We follow this with some examples of interventions (a list that is by no means exhaustive). Finally, we close Part IV and the book with a description of some of the blocks to effective interventions. It has been our experience that novice, and even veteran, group therapists most frequently experience difficulty conceptualizing and determining which interventions to employ. We hope that this section will help leaders become more spontaneous and responsive as they lead their groups.

CONTENTS

PART III

Group Stages   53

PART IV

Interventions 81

PART I

GROUP PROCESS WITHIN A SYSTEMS FRAMEWORK AND THE THREE ELEMENTS THAT CONSTITUTE A GROUP

Historically, most group therapy models developed out of individual psychotherapy. This means that, essentially, therapists conducted individual therapy within a group setting. Hence the crucial elements for change were limited to the dynamics of the interaction between therapist and client. It is our belief, however, that if group therapy is to be an effective system for change, it is necessary to escape from these beginnings and to think of it as a social system. What distinguishes systemic interactive group therapy from individual therapy is the presence of group processes. It is the recognition and management of these processes, along with an understanding of how they are generated and how they influence group development, that enable group leaders to be effective. In the following pages, we introduce you to a systems approach to interactive group therapy, the three subsystems or elements that make up the group, and the seven primary group processes that are generated by the interaction among the elements.

GENERAL SYSTEMS THEORY

Our perception of group therapy as a social system has its roots in General Systems Theory, which was developed by the biologist Ludwig von Bertalanffy (1968). Bertalanffy believed that scientific thinking had become reductionist in attempting to explain phenomena, so he set out to challenge the microapproach to scientific inquiry—that is, the position that in order to understand phenomena, it was best to reduce them to their smallest parts and study those parts in isolation. Bertalanffy's challenge to this view, which was prevalent in the 1940s, insisted that the way to understand seemingly unrelated events was not to isolate their parts, but rather to place them in a context where they could be viewed as parts of a larger system. Thus he introduced General Systems Theory (GST).

To Bertalanffy, a living system was one whose parts were in dynamic interaction. He held that the way to grasp how a system works is to observe the interactive processes taking place among the elements that compose it. Those who subscribe to GST thinking, then, consider *how* systems are organized and *how* their parts are interdependently related. Traditional scientific inquiry tended to seek out basic cause-and-effect explanations for phenomena. This linear approach could explain the domino effect—for example, domino 1 falls against domino 2, which causes it to fall against domino 3, which causes it, in turn, to fall against domino 4, and so on. Adherents of GST, in contrast, are more concerned with the interactive pattern formed by the relationship of the parts within the system or among systems than with the parts themselves (Nichols & Schwartz, 1994). Thus the *process* of the interactive patterns becomes the focus of study.

To envision what is meant here, imagine that you just fell against the person standing next to you, who, in turn, fell against the person standing next to him or her. It is likely there will be some kind of interaction among all three of you. Precisely what kind of interaction cannot be predicted, but the phenomenon will lead to an interactive pattern(s) among all of you. Bertalanffy would have us focus on the interactive pattern(s) of this three-person system rather than isolate each person and study that individual independently of the other two. Now, if the interactive patterns among the three of you were studied over time, what would be learned and understood would be the process—that is, the *how* and *why*—of your interactions collectively.

Group therapists such as H. Durkin (1981) and Agazarian and Janoff (1993) have introduced systems thinking into group therapy in recent decades. Group therapists who *think systematically* realize that it is the group as a whole that needs to be addressed. They perceive the group as being more than a gathering of eight or nine individuals. They focus on the interactive patterns of the subsystems that make up the group, on how each of the subsystems interacts with the group as a whole, and on how the group as a whole interacts with each of the subsystems. In other words, group therapists who think systemically are conscious of "circular causality." For example, when they intervene with one member, they are aware that they need to consider the effect that intervention will have on every other member of the group, on the group as a whole, and ultimately on themselves as group leaders. Group therapists who think systematically believe that it is shortsighted to perceive member A's issue in isolation of other members' issues, the leader, and the whole group.

To sum up, systemically thinking leaders do not observe events that occur within the group in isolation, but rather in terms of their interdependence and the subsequent patterned responses these events evoke in each of the subsystems over time.

THREE-ELEMENT SYSTEM

It is our view that every therapy group consists of three subsystems, which we refer to as *elements*. These three elements are the member, the leader, and the group. Each is equally important to the group process.

Since we view therapy groups as living social systems, it follows that we believe the relationships between and among these elements can best be understood as functions of the total system rather than in isolation. Consequently, we insist that the student of group therapy focus on the transactional processes that occur among and between the elements of the group. It is our contention that you cannot understand the dynamic interactive process of the group using linear thinking because there are no simple cause-and-effect relationships within a therapy group.

Given that therapy groups are living social systems, wherever the therapist makes an intervention, its effect will be felt upon the rest of the system. In other words, regardless of which of the three elements the therapist chooses to affect, each of the other two elements will also be affected. Since to touch one element is to touch all three, the therapist needs to carefully consider how an intervention will affect not only the element being focused upon but also the other two.

Our application of General Systems Theory to therapy groups also suggests that groups have their own self-regulating processes, the function of which is to maintain the status quo, or homeostasis, of the group. Therefore efforts to bring about change in any one of the elements will be resisted. It follows that no change or growth can occur without the introduction of conflict and the creation of a state of disequilibrium.

The disharmony that sets the stage for system change will surely result in anxiety, so the recognition of and management of anxiety is central to effective group leadership. It is therefore essential that group therapists learn to accept and deal with anxiety. Therapists who seek to avoid or ignore anxiety will be incapable of effecting growth in the therapy groups they lead.

We have said that group therapy occurs as the result of the interactive process among the leader, the individual members, and the group as a whole, and that it is therefore essential to consider all three of these elements in relationship to one another and to realize that their interdependence means a change in one element will effect a change in the other two. This leads us to a corollary view: Interactions among the three elements are required to release group processes such as contagion, conflict, anxiety, consensual validation, universality, family reenactment, and instillation of hope. In fact, what distinguishes interactive group therapy from individual therapy is the very presence of these group processes. In order to recognize and manage these processes, the group therapist must understand how they originate and how they influence group development.

Types of Group Processes

Contagion

One member's behavior within the group generally elicits other group processes. For instance, a member of one of our groups began in one session to talk about her sense of "emptiness." The more she described her emptiness, the more attentive and involved other members became—all sat forward in their chairs, some cried or gave other evidence of being touched deeply. One male member of the group who saw himself as unattractive, yet was attracted to the woman talking about her emptiness, began to rock back and forth in his chair. Then, suddenly, he propelled himself out of his seat, went down on his knees, held the woman's hand, and began crying. By talking in such a way about her "emptiness," the woman had acted as an emotional stimulant to the entire group, eliciting *emotional contagion* and generating for one male member a *corrective emotional experience*. For the moment, this member forgot his view of himself as unattractive and allowed himself to engage in an act from which he would normally have refrained.

Conflict

Becoming experientially involved in a group leads inevitably to conflict. Generally, conflict affects each element at varying degrees of intensity throughout the life stages of the group. Issues that generate conflict are usually existential matters such as significance, authority, autonomy, attraction, intimacy, dependence, growth, change, power, control, and loss. These kinds of issues cut across and through each of the three elements of the group: they have no boundaries. Neither the group, individual members, nor the leader is exempt. The experience of conflict, in fact, is what the leader has in common with the members and with the group as a whole. The difference is that the leader has to have come to terms with the issues that generate conflict. Only by acknowledging their existence can the leader recognize what provides the emotional intensity that ultimately fuels the therapeutic process.

Whitaker and Liebermann (1964) have proposed a paradigm for conceptualizing the employment of conflict in the therapeutic process. They refer to this paradigm as the *focal conflict model*. Its configuration is shown in Figure 1.

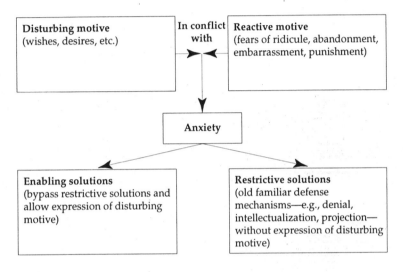

FIGURE 1   Focal Conflict Model

Let us first apply the focal conflict model to the *individual member's* behavior. *Disturbing motives* are the member's private agenda, wishes, desires, or secrets that are in conflict with *reactive motives* or fears, such as ridicule, embarrassment, and abandonment. The member may wish to reveal his or her disturbing motive, but at the same time is fearful of being punished or laughed at or incurring some other fearful consequence. The conflict between the disturbing and reactive motive produces anxiety in the member. Since anxiety can be tolerated for only short periods of time, the member usually adopts a solution to get rid of the anxiety generated by the conflict. The solution may take on one of two forms: restrictive or enabling.

Restrictive solutions are a member's defensive mechanisms. Faced with intolerable anxiety, the member will resort to familiar solutions, such as intellectualization, denial, or projection. These restrictive solutions are designed to relieve the member's anxiety as well as to reduce the member's projected motives, or fears. Consequently, resorting to a restrictive solution precludes verbal expression of the disturbing motive. In contrast, an *enabling solution* bypasses the member's reactive fear and allows for at least some expression of the disturbing motive.

The focal conflict model can also be applied to *leader* and *group* behavior. For instance, a leader who wishes to reveal personal feelings regarding the behavior of a group member or of the whole group (disturbing motive) may be too fearful of the member's or the group's disapproval to do so (reactive motive). The leader, then, adopts a restrictive solution to relieve the anxiety engendered by holding simultaneously disturbing and reactive motives.

To examine group behavior in focal conflict terms, let us assume that a member of a therapy group expresses suicidal thoughts in the first group session (disturbing motive). The group's response to this expression of suicidal intention may be the restrictive solution of denial (group defense). Thus the expression of suicidal thoughts by one member elicits a focal conflict for every other member and, collectively, for the entire group. The group behavior of denial is a function of the anxiety elicited by the member's declaration of intention to commit suicide. It is also a function of the collective group's fear of intensifying the suicidal member's intention or fear of its incompetence in assisting the member or fear of punishment by the therapist, who is the only figure competent to handle the suicidal member. In such a case, it is possible that both the group and the leader will engage in denial (collusion). The leader might be as frightened and anxious as the collective group and therefore avoid the member expressing suicidal wishes, suggest a private session with that member, or change the subject.

The focal conflict model encourages us to understand the behavior of the leader, member, and group as interdependent. Further, it suggests that during the course of a session, a series of sessions, or the life of the group, each element has a bearing on the other elements and that the elements are integrated in the form of either a static or a changing system.

There is one important difference between Whitaker and Liebermann's focal conflict model and our own model, and that is that Whitaker and Liebermann place primary emphasis on group behavior, whereas we see each element of the therapy group as having *equal* importance for the group's growth and development.

Anxiety

Anxiety in a therapy group is a state of continual tension resulting from our unsuccessful attempts to cope with internal conflicts whose roots lie in earlier conflicts occurring in our first group—our family of origin. When confronted by issues presented in a therapy group—for example, when a member reveals that she was abused by her father—I may experience internal rumbling inside my stomach or a sudden sense of panic. The more the other members talk about the issue, the stronger my tension becomes. In an effort to make this tension go away, I may try to change the subject, attack the talking member, ignore that member, detach myself from the group, talk about the subject of abuse intellectually, or use some other restrictive solution to dispel my anxiety. My goal then, is to establish a group condition that will reduce my discomfort. If in this manner I am successful in reducing my tension, I will have interfered with another member's learning, the group's development, and my own growth as well. I will have detrimentally influenced the behavior of all three elements of the group in order to diminish my anxiety—anxiety that is a necessary condition of learning.

If, instead, I permit myself to listen openly to the other member, fully experience and acknowledge my anxiety by talking about abuse, I make anxiety my teacher. In the early sessions of the group, I may not talk openly about the anxiety I am experiencing. Rather, I may look away, move my feet, shake, cough, or whatever—all gestures indicating that I am distressed. However, if I prod myself to talk about what I am feeling in response to the other member, I will be taking a step in the right direction. As I result, I may feel some relief and perhaps acquire some understanding concerning the source of my anxiety. Was I abused at home myself? Was I neglected? Do I feel anxious because a female member is talking? Does she remind me of my mother, sister, wife? What is it? I may not find out the answers immediately, but at least I will have opened myself to discovering them in subsequent sessions. Because I tolerated my anxiety and talked about it, I *contributed* to the other members' growth. By allowing the anxiety present in the group to exist, I did not impede the group's development. And I did not fall apart nor incur terrible consequences.

To illustrate how one member's behavior can elicit intermittent anxiety over many group sessions for the co-leaders, the other members, and the group as a whole, let us consider the behavior of a member of an outpatient therapy group one of us was leading.

By the 11th session of this group, it had become evident that whenever Jeff discussed his concerns about dating women, he would cover his private parts with his hands. It was obvious that the co-leaders as well as the other group members were aware of this automatic action on Jeff's part, but the issue was ignored by all of us.

The leaders and members had a disturbing motive (wishing to comment on Jeff's behavior) that conflicted with their reactive motive (embarrassing themselves or hurting Jeff's feelings). The group and the leaders were, to a varying extent, clearly anxious. Still, each time the event occurred, they enacted a restrictive solution by avoiding comments that might have made Jeff aware of a behavior that was interfering with his relationships with women and that probably was a key to important related issues, such as his sexuality in general, his religion, and his family influences. Moreover, members who had issues similar to Jeff's remained untouched; thus, even as they failed to help Jeff grow, they were cutting themselves off from growth. The group's way of dealing with Jeff's issues was: "We can't talk about sexuality overtly displayed by a group member." Thus the group adopted a restrictive solution that bypassed the meaning of Jeff's behavior.

As the sessions continued, Jeff's behavior and the anxiety it aroused in the rest of us did not die out. As for the leaders, Jeff's behavior disturbed us enough so that we talked about it outside the group and discussed our unwillingness to confront it within the group. We knew that it was important to raise the issue within the group, but we disagreed as to who should do so. My position was that since my co-therapist was Jeff's primary therapist, she should raise the issue. She, in turn, felt this was the kind of issue that was best approached by a male therapist.

Finally, early on in session 14, I addressed the matter of Jeff's covering his private parts in the group. As the group solution was made visible, anxiety surfaced. Jeff acknowledged his behavior, and other members expressed their reactions to it. We then engaged in an intellectual discussion of displays of sexuality—an effort by the group to find a less restrictive solution to the issues generated by the exposure of Jeff's behavior. As the session progressed, however, members began talking about related behaviors they had observed or used to distance members of the opposite sex. Members were supportive of Jeff, though he remained rather quiet as this information was revealed. Thus the group was able to tolerate extended periods of anxiety about sexuality by talking about it both personally and intellectually—consequently providing a more enabling solution to discussions regarding sexual feelings.

From this example, we can draw several conclusions about the role of anxiety and its impact on group process.

First, specific issues or themes relevant to members' concerns can arouse anxiety in all three elements of the therapy group. Second, either member(s), leader(s), or the entire group will attempt to reduce the level of anxiety by enacting restrictive solutions.

Third, anxiety should generally be distributed among group members rather than vested in one member. Note that the distribution of anxiety about Jeff's behavior in the 14th session led to a less restrictive solution, which, in turn, led to a new group norm permitting more open discussion of sexual issues.

Finally, anxiety is a mobilizer of group process. The more distributed and intense the anxiety, the more evident the solutions acted out by group members will be. In this process, more therapeutic data and clues will become available to the group therapist.

A group that has minimal anxiety will typically develop minimal interactions and involvement. Without tension, a therapy group will be of little use to members because it will become dominated by restrictive and a very few enabling solutions.

For change to occur in therapy groups, the three elements must become capable of tolerating increasing periods of anxiety so that all will see that their fears of disastrous consequences are fantasies. The recognition and management of anxiety are therefore central to effective group leadership. Group therapists need to learn to feel comfortable with anxiety, for if they run from it or choose not to turn toward it, they will miss the opportunity to use this primary force for change.

Consensual Validation

One of the most important reasons for engaging in group therapy is that it provides an opportunity that is unavailable in individual psychotherapy. That is, group therapy allows one to check out one's behavior with several other persons and to receive feedback from an entire group rather than a single individual. One receives from the group honest assessments against which self-assessments may be cross-checked. The therapy group provides this advantage over any other group (family, work, play) one belongs to because its members have no ulterior motives or agendas. The primary function of the group is to help individuals gain the interpersonal skills to cope effectively with their other social environments.

The same holds true for the therapist and the group as a whole. Within a group setting, the therapist's views may be openly called into question. It is an important moment when authority figures are challenged as to their purpose in the group. Similarly, the group as a whole can be challenged by individual members or the leaders as to the facilitative value of its behaviors. As a result of being forced to meet such challenges, the leader or the group receives consensual validation. In no other type of therapeutic relationship is this kind of validation possible.

Universality

The notion that all human beings are similar is not new. However, people seeking therapy invariably ask us whether we think their problems are unique. What they are really expressing is a belief in their own singularity: Because of an intensely personal conflict, they feel as though they are different from others. Although Yalom (1985) finds this phenomenon quite typical, he also points out that the members of a therapy group discover much common ground once they begin to interact. It is therefore important for leaders to use all their skills in getting members to interact among themselves; in fact, the more leaders can help members recognize the universality of their experiences and feelings during the early stages of the group, the more they can facilitate group unity.

Family Reenactment

A group member's family of origin and childhood conflicts will always influence his or her behavior in the group. In many ways, the group resembles a family: Co-leaders represent the authority of parent figures, and members represent siblings. It is quite common to observe and expect that members will replay their roles from old family scripts, especially when they have unresolved issues with authority. For people to see the therapist as a parent figure and to call up old coping mechanisms in dealing with the therapist is not unusual. Sibling rivalries and the only-child syndrome are also often played out against the backdrop of the group.

Leaders who recognize these family reenactments are in a good position to help members work through old emotional impasses and unfinished family business. They do this by having the members test out new approaches to dealing with these issues in the group. By helping members adopt a more here-and-now focus, leaders can wean them from living in the past and engaging in there-and-then behaviors in their current interactions with members, leaders, and people outside the group.

Instillation of Hope

Some years ago when one of us was taking a course in family therapy, the instructor emphasized the need for the therapeutic process to include the instillation of hope. How often have we heard a statement along the lines of "I guess you must think my case is pretty hopeless" from a client? People who go into therapy are usually feeling quite hopeless. Most have already made many attempts to solve their problem(s) and have failed. These clients view therapy as a last resort. The task of the leaders is to believe in the value of their work and in the power of the group (Yalom, 1985). As members of the group manage to come to terms with their own issues, they will model success for others in the group.

PART II

FACTORS INFLUENCING LEADER, MEMBER, AND GROUP BEHAVIORS

The group as a whole comprises a series of interactive processes between and among the three elements. Affecting these processes at the elemental level are a number of factors. The following pages present the most significant of these factors and show how and why understanding their impact is essential to effective group leadership.

SYSTEMS OF COMMUNICATION

*Group therapy has many systems
of nonverbal communication that influence
leader, member, and group behaviors.*

Foulkes (1964) once stated that "The process of communication has impressed the present writer more and more as basic for the understanding of group dynamics" (p. 80). His statement highlights one of our convictions regarding group therapy: that there are many systems of communication that pervade the group process and impinge upon leader, member, and group behaviors.

In our experience with psychotherapy groups, *how* people behave (process) is more important than *what* (content) they say, particularly in the early stages of group development. Early in group life, members do not freely articulate their concerns, thoughts, and feelings. Instead, they usually mask their private thoughts and feelings by employing restrictive solutions or coping mechanisms designed to deal with their fears. A more valid and reliable index of members' thoughts and feelings at this stage of group life is their *actions* or the *manner* in which they communicate.

The behavior of beginning group therapists tends to parallel that of members. That is, new group leaders are also prone to be intimidated by the group therapy process to the point where true expression of their thoughts and feelings is inhibited. Again, their actions are a more accurate index of their thoughts and feelings regarding member or group behavior than their words are.

Group behavior is more difficult to "read" than either member or leader behavior since it is rarely verbalized. There are exceptions. Scapegoating, for example, is one of the "loudest" forms of group verbalizations, and it certainly influences leader and member behavior. Group denial is a "quiet" form of group verbalization, but its passivity has a strong effect on the group as well. Learning to "read" group behavior is an important task for the beginning group therapist—and even for the experienced therapist, who may at times ignore or minimize its influence to the detriment of group development.

In this section, we examine several nonverbal communication systems that characterize therapy groups and describe how these systems influence the three elements. All of these communication systems are identified by actions rather than words.

Proxemics

Proxemics refers to the emotional and physical distance between and among members and leaders. This can be determined by observing where members and leaders sit in relation to one another over time. Tracking which members and leaders come late or early to sessions can also be revealing. In keeping with our model, we will examine proxemics in terms of leader, member, and group behavior.

The seating position the *leader* assumes in relation to other group members not only reflects the leader's own comfort level with intimacy but also has a bearing on the closeness group members will establish with one another as well as with the group as a whole. Often the distance established by the leader is reflected in the distance members establish among themselves, at least initially. The distance a therapist assumes from members can eliminate the possibility of physical touch between leader and nearby members. Thus leaders can convey a *group norm* regarding "touching" behavior by their seating position in the group. In taking a more distant stance, they are setting limits on the intimacy boundaries they will tolerate and eliminating a potential source of valuable nonverbal communication data. Leaders who discourage physical closeness are depriving themselves of the opportunity to observe members' comfort or discomfort regarding touching behavior.

Leaders can encourage closeness by, prior to the group session, arranging chairs so that they are fairly close together. The group norm of closeness will be enhanced by the smaller distances between leaders and members. True, one consequence of close seating patterns early in the group's life is often anxiety on the part of members about the unnatural closeness expected in this new relationship. However, this is more than offset by the opportunity to *see* what members do in relation to the preestablished closeness—a form of nonverbal communication that tells the leader how each member is used to behaving in an intimate setting.

To sum up, a leader's own comfort with intimacy is reflected in the degree of distance that leader maintains from group members and the group, and the leader's example in this area can elicit or cut off the kind of nonverbal data that can lead to greater group intimacy.

Proxemics provide the leader with a rich source of data regarding members' behavior. The distance that one member occupies in contrast to that of other members can "tell" us that member's level of comfort with others in the group. For instance, a male member may choose to sit only next to the men in the group and distance himself from the women. Or a group member may sit directly opposite the leader for purposes of "observing" the leader. Another member may prefer to sit at the "right hand of the authority" to ensure protection or favorable regard by the leader. Still another member may sit at such a distance from everyone else as to be isolated or "outside" the group. All of these *actions* tell the leader something about client concerns that may be unstated verbally. However, a leader should be sure that a member exhibits a *consistent* pattern over a small number of sessions before considering this information valid and reliable.

To illustrate, one of the authors recounts an experience as a member of a therapy group:

> As a member of a therapy group, I remember when my "seating" behavior provided the therapist with very clear nonverbal data regarding my unexpressed feelings toward another group member called Jim. For approximately 3 weeks, I had strong negative feelings toward Jim. I could not pinpoint my source of anger and dislike for him. As each week passed by, the intensity of my feelings increased to the point that I did not want to attend group. I had,

during these successive weeks, managed to sit as far as possible from Jim, thus reducing my intense feelings. This required my arriving early to group to find my "seat." On the fourth week, I arrived late, only to find one seat left, that being the closest to Jim. I refused the chair and sat on the floor as far as possible from Jim. Clearly, even a beginning therapist would have noticed my "observable" behavior and commented upon it. My actions and consequent distance emerged clearly without verbal disclosure. By commenting on my behavior, the leader "prompted" me to *begin* verbalizing my thoughts and feelings regarding Jim, which I had successfully avoided doing up to that point.

Proxemics also provides clues regarding group behavior. Distances between members and between members and the leader can tell us how safe members feel with the group. Earliness or lateness in arriving at group sessions can tell us how important or how attractive the group is to some or all of its members. The greater the distance between group members, the less likely they are to reveal their personal thoughts and feelings and the more likely they are to engage in restrictive solutions such as group denial and intellectualization. Group therapists should look to their own feelings toward each group they lead for clues about that group's proxemics. In our experience, each group we conduct has a distinct personality. We often find ourselves more excited about meeting with one group as opposed to another. We may arrive just on time for one group, and be a half an hour early for another. What do these actions tell us about how we feel and think about the behavior of each group? Perhaps, like some group members, we are feeling distant from one group and very attracted to and safe with another.

Whatever the case, the group's proxemics establishes a norm that influences member and leader behavior.

Unconscious Behavior

Unconscious behavior, or behavior that is not manifest to the leader, the member, or the group, is another type of communication that affects the course and development of group therapy. Recounting dreams—unconscious material par excellence—and exploring their meaning in a therapy group can provide insights and valuable data to group members. Group therapists vary in their opinions on exploring dreams in the context of group therapy; many would restrict dream work to individual therapy. In any case, there are other unconscious behaviors that affect member, leader, and group behaviors, and these can profitably be explored in a group setting. An example of such behavior and how it can impact on the therapy group follows.

Jay, a member of an outpatient therapy group, talked at one session about his fears regarding impotence and his inability to maintain an erection. Female members of the group tended to be supportive and understanding, but male members were generally unable to identify with Jay and expressed little understanding of his concerns. The group leader, however, was supportive of Jay. The following week, Jay did not come to the session, and there was no message explaining his absence. The group as a whole took no notice of Jay's absence during the entire session (unconscious behavior), until the leader commented on it near the end of the session. Members then expressed surprise that Jay was missing, but no one mentioned the content of his concerns as revealed the previous week. Jay returned the following week, and no one commented on his absence the previous week until the leader questioned him. Jay replied that he had "forgotten" the group was meeting (unconscious member behavior).

Clearly, Jay had repressed the discomfort created in him by the other male members' lack of support, understanding, or identification with his sexual concerns, and this discomfort had caused him to skip a session with no conscious awareness of why he had done so. Member behavior "matched" Jay's unconscious repression and resulted in group repression even when his absence was noted by the therapist in the second session. Further, the members and the group missed the opportunity to express their thoughts and feelings regarding other forms of impotence they experienced in their jobs and their relationships within and outside the group. The leader's behavior during the three sessions—delaying in examining group events, not talking about impotence, and so on—contributed to the unconscious behavior of the group and the members. Thus the unconscious behavior (denial) manifested by the group, the members, and the leader constituted a system of communication that resulted in missed opportunities and the enactment of very restrictive norms around the issues of impotence and sexuality in general. The group was not a "safe" place to talk about these issues. The need to prevent unconscious behavior from becoming a system of communication permeating the group was ignored. Consequently, the opportunity to verbally express disturbing motives (thoughts and feelings) aroused by overt events was lost. In focal-conflict terms, Jay expressed a disturbing motive that resulted in denial by the other men in the group, and subsequently by the entire group and, to a lesser extent, by the leader. The group's avoidance of the issue/ theme increased Jay's already intense discomfort and caused him to miss a session and resulted in the repression of material important to himself and other members. The group had entered into a state of disequilibrium, manifested by high levels of anxiety, and restored its equilibrium by group denial and repression of important thoughts and feelings regarding impotence.

Tense of Self-Disclosure

The tense used in a self-disclosure reveals the level of comfort or discomfort that the member, leader, or group is experiencing at the moment of disclosure. In the next section is a model that defines five levels of disclosure as a function of tense. One assumption of this model is that self-disclosure, regardless of the tense used, is related to the content and process current within the group at the moment of disclosure.

Model of Self-Disclosure

1. *Nonverbal Self-Disclosure:* Thoughts and feelings on a covert level related to the content and process occurring within the group, but disclosed nonverbally.

2. *There-and-Then Self-Disclosure:* Disclosures related to the content and process occurring within the group, but drawn from the distant past.

3. *Here-and-Then Self-Disclosure:* Disclosures related to the content and process occurring within the group, but drawn from the recent past.

4. *Here-and-Now Disclosure:* Disclosures related to the content and process occurring within the group.

5. *Catharsis:* Disclosures related to the content and process occurring within the group that manifest a loss of control.

The tense of a self-disclosure generally influences the degree of intensity and discomfort group members experience upon hearing the communication. Moreover, the group response (group behavior) in terms of tense is an index of the group's level of comfort with the communication.

Using the example of Jay's revelation of his difficulties in sexual relationships to the group, let us say that Jay disclosed his impotence in the recent past (a there-and-then self-disclosure) and his fear that it might occur in his current relationships. This tense caused extreme discomfort in the members, the group, and the leader. If Jay had introduced his concern in the context of the distant past (a there-and-then self-disclosure), the members, group, and leader would almost certainly have experienced less intense discomfort and felt "safer" about "opening up"—at least to a minimal extent.

Whenever the tense of a self-disclosure moves close to the present, the "ante" goes up and members are less likely to reveal themselves. For that reason, members sometimes move even further back than to the there-and-then by employing the third person. Jay might have introduced the issue of impotence, for instance, by saying "I have a friend who's having problems with impotence and wants some advice," and then advanced into the here-and-then. The inherent threat of a discomforting topic like impotence to member, leader, and group is reduced by increasing the distance from the here-and-then.

As the group develops, the communication tense usually moves increasingly toward the present, or the here-and-now, because the group feels safer and more intimate to members. Our experience suggests that with the increasing adoption of the here-and-now by members and leader, new issues emerge that can be threatening to express in the present tense. Thus, even in advanced groups, the communication style of members, leader, and group may revert back to the there-and-then. We believe that such divergences into the past have a place in even the most advanced groups and must be tolerated. For instance, a member of a two-year-old open-ended group one of us led revealed a history of suicide attempts. This was news to the group members and a novel theme for the group. Though the information presented was in the there-and-then, the group's response was distant (there were long silences). Furthermore, the group behaved like a beginning group, waiting for the leader to "manage" this new event.

Past, Present, and Future Communications

Communication tense can also be used by the leader as a diagnostic tool as well as for a host of interventions. In assessing the communication style of an individual member or the whole group, it is helpful to determine the extent to which it reflects the past, the present, and the future. It is our experience that references to the future are very minimal in the early stages of group development. Rather, communications overwhelmingly reflect the past and, to some extent, the present. We have also found that even in more *mature* groups member and group communications infrequently touch on the future, and when they do, the attitude tends to be one of bleakness or fantasy. Nonetheless, we believe that the future tense is as rich a source of data regarding member and group behavior as the past and present tenses are. Diagnostically, it is helpful for assessing individual members' attitudes toward life, death, immortality, spirituality, separation from the past, and the current therapy group, as well as feelings about abandonment. It provides important clues about the readiness of members to leave the therapy group. It is our contention that members should be able to examine and integrate the past, present, and future openly within the group before leaving the group. This is particularly true for members of open-ended or time-unlimited therapy groups.

With regard to group behavior, use of the future tense is a good barometer of the group's growth, maturity, and ability to tolerate future communications.

A group's success or failure in encountering and communicating concerns regarding the future is largely contingent on the *leader's* comfort and/or discomfort with the future. Leaders who feel reasonably comfortable about their own existence and place in the world and who can regard the issues of death and immortality with a fair degree of equanimity will be able to reinforce members' comments about the future. They will also be willing to introduce the "future" into the group and to examine the group's resistance to talking about it. This emphasis helps members to speak openly about their concerns (past and present) regarding their future life. On the other hand, leaders who exhibit denial of the future insulate individual members and the group as a whole from encountering, examining, and learning about themselves. Successful discussions of the future allow members to see that the future is not necessarily frightening.

Actually, the future is an undeniable reality, which for some group members is a source of *anxiety*, and for others an important source of *motivation*. In either case, communications about the future are a valuable data source for the member, the leader, and the group. For those experiencing anxiety, such discussions are an opportunity to examine old or recurrent conflicts in light of how they are hampering current and future life. They may find that their fears are exaggerated. For members who are already motivated to go forward, such discussions are a further impetus to take their place in the world. They are encouraged to discover their true priorities in life, what they want out of current and future relationships, what legacies they desire to bequeath to loved ones or friends, and how to prepare for their own death.

A man we shall call Frank provides a good illustration of what past, present, and future communications can reveal about a group member and, consequently, about the entire group. When Frank entered group at the age of 60, he had been separated from his wife for 12 years and had been living with another woman for 5 years. He was severely depressed. During the seventh session, he disclosed that the woman he was living with was pressing him to divorce his wife and marry her; if he refused, she was planning to leave him. As he revealed himself to the group, Frank couched his statements in the present tense —"I don't know what to do"—and in the future tense —"If I do as she wants, then I'll have to let go of my family. If I don't do as she asks, I'm afraid I'll grow old alone. After all, it isn't easy for a man my age to find someone."

Two central themes for this group were fear of abandonment and fear of being alone. As Frank continued to talk about his dilemma, his disclosures drew responses from other members that indicated they identified with his plight and that they, too, were fearful of facing life alone. The anxiety accompanying their disclosures was quite intense.

Recognizing that the group *as a whole* was struggling with the fear of aloneness, my co-leader described to the group the effect that Frank's disclosure seemed to be having on it. She followed that by stating to the group that Frank was revealing, not only his fears of aloneness and abandonment, but also his fear of aging (mortality). She added that perhaps these were issues that the whole group might be having difficulty with, and that since these concerns were now in the open, it might be a good idea to discuss them.

The direction the group's discussion then took addressed members' fears of ultimately living and dying alone, with no one caring for them. Frank, for instance, was afraid that marrying his companion would result in the loss of his family, and that this meant that he might not be remembered and thus his existence would have been in vain. The co-leader's response conveyed her security with these themes because she had come to terms with them for herself. This communication told members that such matters could be addressed and tolerated by the leader, which, in turn, led to the group as a whole tolerating and addressing them.

Emotional Intensity

Emotional intensity is a system of communication that can be *seen* or *heard* that expresses the level of discomfort experienced by each of the three elements in response to events occurring in a therapy group. *Modulation of affect* refers to the strength or intensity of a person's emotional response to an event in the group; it tells us how important that event is to the person. The more intense the affect revealed in the person's verbal or nonverbal response to the event, the more likely that event has meaning and therapeutic value to that person and warrants examination by the group.

Emotional intensity is manifested both verbally and nonverbally. Modulations in voice patterns are the primary verbal indicator of emotional intensity. The following transaction, which occurred in one of our groups, is an example of verbal display of emotional intensity.

A member suddenly announced he was gay. Another member's response was, "Oh my God, I didn't know we'd have one of *them* in this group!" The level of this man's felt discomfort was plainly evidenced by the strength of his verbal response to the announcement. Feelings, then, are evaluators of thoughts. Conversely, a member who speaks quietly, mumbles to himself and "monitors" his response may be experiencing an equally strong response.

Nonverbal emotional intensity is evidenced in a variety of behavioral responses often referred to as *body language*. For example, eye movements (opening and shutting, intense gazing or focusing, looking forward or away from a member) often reveal the emotional effect of an event on a member. To return to the example of the man who announced he was gay, a group member who had a strong reaction to the announcement might have displayed this by an increase in pupil size. Other examples of nonverbal emotional intensity in response to an uncomfortable issue presented in group are leg and hand movements.

Leaders who pay close attention to the felt discomfort displayed by members and the group will be able to discern which issues tend to disturb which members. They will also have a valuable tool for understanding members' concerns without having to prompt members to verbalize those concerns. In fact, they will note when members are "acting out" specific issues that hinder their interpersonal relationships.

The emotional intensity of the entire group is often manifested by a group behavior known as *denial*. To return to the example of Jay, the member who disclosed his impotence to the group, the group's subsequent refusal to acknowledge his absence from the following session was a form of denial of discomfort with the issue of impotence. Had the group's discomfort with Jay's revelation been even more intense, this might have been manifested by the absence of other members, as well as Jay, the following week. Such a scenario would indicate both group and specific member discomfort.

Leaders are also subject to verbal and nonverbal manifestations of emotional intensity. For instance, when Jay discussed his impotence, my internal discomfort was manifested by my silence and refusal to comment on the obvious lack of support Jay was receiving from the other men in the group. When Jay stayed away from the following session, had I continued to collude with the group in avoiding the subject of his absence, I would have helped perpetuate group and member discomfort with this issue. Furthermore, the greater my discomfort, the less likely I would be to see and hear variations in group and member emotional intensity. Consequently, my denial would have reduced anxiety (including my own), which is a primary force for change in group therapy, and thereby decreased the ability of members and the group to tolerate necessary levels of anxiety during the life of the group. In effect, I would have been enacting a restrictive solution regarding the discussion of impotence and related issues.

Silence: Group as a Whole

"You cannot not communicate: Silence is communication" (Swogger, 1981). When the group as a whole is silent, it is saying something to the leaders and to each of the members. The task of leaders is to understand and interpret what the group is expressing through its silence. At times, group silence is to be perceived as an act of resistance, as nonproductive or destructive; at other times, it should be seen as productive, active, and constructive—a time for reflection and introspection (Carroll & Wiggins, 1990; Heider, 1985; Jacobs et al., 1994; Kottler, 1994; Trotzer, 1977). New leaders frequently perceive all group silences as threatening events; they do not have enough experience to discern which silences are natural and expected consequences of group process. In attending to *when* and *how* silence occurs, leaders are taking the first steps toward understanding whether or not a silence is productive.

Is the silence occurring the first session? Or in the 12th? Have norms been established to build a group culture that allows members to feel safe about self-disclosure? How is the group composed? Have you as leader been authoritarian in your interactions? What in the history of the group could be contributing to the group silence? For instance, did a member leave the group prematurely? Was the previous week's session intensely emotional? Does the group as a whole have a common pregroup history that is contributing to this silence? How clear are group goals? Has a member just made a deep emotional disclosure? Have you as leader offered process illumination of the group as a whole? How much extragroup socializing—that is, subgrouping—has been going on? Has the group just finished some work and is therefore in transition? Is the group facing its final session—that is, termination?

As you can see, there are a great number of possible reasons for group silence. Remember, silence can be a moment when ambiguity is very present. Leaders need to be sensitive not only to the amount of ambiguity the group can tolerate but also to the amount they themselves are capable of tolerating. All too often, we have observed our students prematurely break a group silence because they have a low tolerance for moments of ambiguity. On the other hand, Jacobs and colleagues (1994) suggest that when members seem overly perplexed or anxious, leaders should not allow a silence to continue beyond 15–20 seconds. They contend that extensive periods of silence—that is, 5 minutes or longer—are counterproductive in therapy groups. Porter (1994) agrees, maintaining that if a group silence persists, it is to be interpreted as an act of resistance.

It is our position that whether a silence is productive or counterproductive, group leaders should consider making a group-as-a-whole intervention that will encourage member response. In doing this, we often rely on the group's common (universal) experience. We have also encouraged our students to strive to discern how they themselves are experiencing the moment and to regard that as parallel to the experience of some, if not all, of the members. We urge them to then make an intervention that links the members together through this common experience. Once a member responds—and eventually one will—you will find you can build off that member's response in a way that draws other members in. Your intention is to encourage the resumption of member-to-member interaction.

For still another view of silence, we refer you to Heider (1985), who encourages leaders to "Allow regular time for silent reflection. Turn inward and digest what has happened. . . . When group members have time to reflect, they can see more clearly what is essential in themselves and others" (p. 23).

The nonverbal communications systems described in this section provide the therapist with a rich source of data relevant to member and group concerns. The beauty of these data for the therapist is that the behaviors in question are *observable* and can be commented on in a *descriptive* fashion— first by leaders, and eventually by group members. In addition, all members "witness" a behavior and can validate descriptions of it by a leader or member. The benefits to the member whose behavior is being described are that the behavior is difficult to deny and the acknowledgment of it is not threatening since it is a concrete and specific datum that is not being "interpreted."

History

The history of individual members, the leader, and the group itself influences the current behaviors and future development of a therapy group.

We use *history* to refer to those member, leader, and group behaviors that have occurred within the group since its inception, and *pregroup history* to refer to the personal histories of the leader and members in other group situations (for example, in family and peer groups) prior to the inception of the therapy group. The pregroup histories of member(s) and leader(s) influence their behavior within the group. In fact, one of our essential assumptions is that a member's behavior within the therapy group reflects his or her behavior in the world outside the group. In other words, people's intergroup behaviors are usually similar to their behaviors in everyday interpersonal situations.

Over the course of many sessions, a member's general style of behavior becomes apparent in the habitual solutions or consistent set of responses that member evidences in dealing with issues that evoke anxiety. For example, a man who is frightened by affectional displays by other members or a leader over a series of sessions might habitually respond by withdrawing, intellectualizing, changing the subject, or remaining silent. The point is, it can be assumed that, in group, members will engage in solutions that give them the greatest sense of comfort and safety. These solutions are tolerable and familiar responses to threatening or anxiety-provoking issues. When a member shifts away from accustomed behavior, it may signal that member is moving beyond habitual responses. This change in one member's historical behavior is bound to affect the behavior of other members in the group—either increasing or decreasing their discomfort, for example.

The history of a therapy group refers to the accumulation of issues, behavior, and affect within the group, as well as the group's response to anxiety-provoking incidents that occur during its life. Content and affect are linked from one session to the next, so that each session is part of a continuum rather than a discrete occurrence. Frequently, it is the accumulation of affect over a series of sessions that generates overwhelming tension within the group, an individual member, or the leader that compels a response requiring change by the therapy group.

Even as the group develops a history over several sessions, so does the leader. Leader history is important both to the individual members and to the entire group. Many members—at least, to some degree—look to the leader for consistency in approach, theory, and interactions. This is especially true early in the group's life. Departures from group or individual expectations can elicit anxiety, undermine trust, and exacerbate fears. To members, the leader is as the anchor who is supposed to forestall harmful consequences in times of perceived threat. Whereas the leader looks for change in member behavior, the members look for stability in leader behavior.

Group leaders see history as a series of benchmarks for each member and for the group as a whole by which they can measure movement. Changes in behavior over sessions may signal movement, maintenance of the status quo, or regression in the group or among individual members. What the leader chooses to do at these critical junctures will influence the current and future operation of the therapy group.

As we have said, the pregroup histories of the leader and the members influence group development. Moreover, the initial session (beginning) of the group creates the earliest history (moment) of the group element, as well as of the other two elements. Along with pregroup history, it plays a vital role in the therapeutic process and the development of the group.

The pregroup history of the *member element* includes family-of-origin experiences, peer-group experiences, work-group experiences, play-group experiences, and previous therapy-group experiences. Leaders should expect members to transfer these previous experiences over into the group. For instance, the leader may draw negative responses from members based on their unresolved conflicts with parents, teachers, and other authority figures. On the other hand, members may react positively to the leader because of positive experiences they have had in relationships with such authority figures. This predisposition to transfer to the leader histories with other authority figures will have an effect on the movement of the group. Such transference is not reserved solely for the leader; it can occur between members as well.

It is also common for individual members to project upon the group, the other members, and the leader their own emotional experiences from former situations. This can either facilitate or inhibit the process of therapy. If the member's projection is based on a negative experience, it may lead to dysfunctional responses such as withdrawing from the group or attacking the leader or other members, or it may take a more passive-aggressive form.

THEMES

What links one therapy session to another and lends continuity to the group are *themes*, or representations of the conscious or unconscious issues individual members, the leader(s), or the group as a whole are dealing with. Authority, affection, intimacy, dependency, and trust are examples of issues that are embedded in themes.

Themes are potential unifiers of the group. In fact, a group's progress or involvement is to a large extent dependent upon the leader's ability to identify and interpret themes presented within the group.

Theme identification and interpretation allow the group to break away from narrowly focused issues. Once an issue has run its course, a group is frequently at a loss as to what to do next. For instance, in a group two of our students were co-leading, a member disclosed that she had just returned from her grandmother's funeral, and then proceeded to share with the group how deeply affected she was by her grandmother's death. A few individual members made empathic overtures to her, but the others remained silent, appearing to be unmoved by her disclosure. Observing the behaviors of the latter, one of the co-leaders remarked on how quiet these members were, and this prompted one of them to say that he could not relate to the issue of death since no one close to him had died. Undaunted by this remark, the co-leader said that maybe the death of an individual had some further meaning, and wondered if the group and this member would want to discuss that. The group was then able to address feelings of loss, powerlessness, and mortality, which carried over to the next few sessions. The group no longer saw death as being one person's issue, but dealt with it as a more universal theme. By broadening the meaning and the context of the issue, the co-leader was able to generate a highly interactive process.

It is important to recognize that what the co-leader did in this case was to attend to how different *members* reacted to a theme, how much energy each member invested in it, and how many members invested any energy in it. By noting the seemingly defensive response of some members—particularly one individual—and how this response was being used to cope with the theme, the co-leader broadened the context of the issue—that is, developed a theme that the other members could identify with. Thus the group was unified and avoided becoming stalemated. Had the co-leader not already come to terms with death herself, it is unlikely the group would have worked through the issues represented by the theme of death.

In another group, the missed opportunity for theme identification was directly related to the co-leaders' unresolved feelings about authority. One of the members repeatedly questioned the co-leaders about their qualifications to lead the group; the co-leaders responded by repeatedly avoiding an answer to the question. The *group as a whole,* which had remained quite passive during the exchanges between the questioning member and the co-leaders, eventually became impatient and expressed anger toward the co-leaders for their failure to be forthright. Thus an impasse was reached in the group, as the opportunity to generate group interaction and develop group unity was missed. During a postgroup supervision session, the co-leaders revealed that they had felt intimidated by the questioner, and later by the entire group. They felt their authority had been challenged, and rather than placing the issue in a broader context, they defended themselves. Had the co-leaders been truly comfortable in their role and had they resolved their own issues concerning authority, they probably would have seen that the real point was not their authority. Rather, it was the need of the challenging member, and subsequently the whole group, to address the issues of trust, safety, security, dependency, intimacy, and the like, as well as the boundaries of authority.

Themes manifest themselves in other ways aside from members voicing their issues. For instance, a leader may observe individual members and the group as a whole engaging in behaviors that convey attraction, hostility, intimacy, or flight from conflict. By seizing upon such opportunities to identify and interpret themes the behaviors are communicating, the leader will generate group interaction. Say, members display defensive behaviors that convey their coping process for managing a specific issue, or that the group as a whole engages in defensive behaviors that convey its means for managing a toxic issue. By acknowledging the behaviors and subsequently identifying and interpreting the themes embedded in them, the leader will help link member to member, unify the group, and establish group cohesiveness.

NORMS AND STANDARDS

*Norms and standards of the group, members,
and leader(s) influence the content and process
of the therapy group and its development.*

Norms refer to the rules that govern behavior in groups, while *standards* refer to the system of punishment and rewards for violating or cooperating with established or evolving rules of behavior. Norms and standards can be explicit and can be determined before the group begins (ground rules of the therapist). Or they can be implicit—that is, evolve consciously or unconsciously during the group's development as a reflection of individual members' or the leader's personal set of norms and standards or the group's collective sense of what the norms and standards should be.

Since no group is exactly like another, it stands to reason that each group will have a unique system of norms and standards. You may find yourself leading three freshmen counseling groups, all matched by age, sex, and group experience, but by the end of the first session, you will discover that each group has a different level of member interaction, participation, and expectations. Moreover, your own response to the group's collective personality will be different in each instance.

Individual members' personal norms and standards vis-à-vis collective group behavior will also vary from group to group. This can be illustrated by watching how members respond to any common incident such as a deep disclosure by a new member. Some groups will "speak" very little, others will support the new member, and still others will attack the new member. In all cases, the members will be reflecting the implicit collective norms and standards of their therapy group.

Another way of conceptualizing *existing* and *developing* norms and standards is to imagine them as providing safety boundaries for the members. The norms and standards of a therapy group exert tremendous influence on member, leader, and group behavior. Conformity to these norms and standards is an important issue, particularly in the early stages of group development. If a group's norms and standards regarding *acceptable behavior* by members are rigid, then the *safety* experienced by members is reduced, their willingness to risk is minimized, and their tendency to conform is increased. (We should note here that many therapists confuse *conformity* with *cohesiveness*; they are not the same.)

Acceptable behavior by group members encompasses *what* (content) can be talked about and *how* (process) it can be talked about during the course of group development. A group's boundaries of acceptable behavior determine its culture—that is, how much conformity/nonconformity will be tolerated within the group. A "good therapy group" is one that evidences, over time, a growing culture, with widening boundaries of acceptable behavior. In other words, it shows greater acceptance of what can be talked about and how, and fosters a growing feeling of safety in members. Figure 2 graphically portrays the impact (evaluation) of a therapy group and its norms and standards.

To illustrate this model, let us recall the therapy session in which a member announced that he was gay. Remember that his revelation prompted one of the other men in the

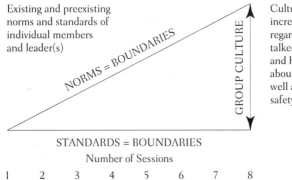

FIGURE 2   Evolution of Norms and Standards

group to shout, "Oh my God, I didn't know we'd have one of *them* in this group!" Some other members displayed nonverbal disapproval, while others remained silent and detached. The boundaries of what could be talked about (content) were being challenged during the very first session. Three members in particular were influenced by their preexisting norms and standards in setting boundaries on the just-evolving *implicit* norms of what could be discussed in group regarding male sexuality and sexuality in general. Moreover, this triad was influencing other members, both male and female, who might have had concerns regarding their sexuality, but were now too frightened to speak out lest they expose themselves to the same disapproval directed at the gay member. Consequently, the perceived safety regarding sexuality experienced by members at this early juncture of the group was defined by a restrictive solution: "We can't talk about sexuality without fear of punishment or disapproval by the group." Clearly, if this evolving implicit norm and standard did not get attention by the leader, it was bound to become explicit.

STAGES

As living social systems, groups have the potential to grow through identifiable stages of development, each of which has its own peculiar qualities. Since, however—consistent with the notion of homeostasis—each stage has its own self-maintenance process, it requires sufficient press (stress) to move the group on to the next stage of development.

There are two major views regarding the stages of group development. One holds that the group develops along a sequential path. This view does not imply the group has a fixed direction, for every group is fluid enough to revert, at times, to an earlier stage—especially if all members have not completed the issues identified with a particular stage.

The other view perceives the group as evolving through a cyclical process—that is, it repeats, from time to time, certain segments or issues from a previous stage. For example, in a long-term group, authority issues occur not only in the first stage, but continuously throughout the group's life. Say a client's issue over authority takes the form of challenging the leader in an early stage. The issue can reappear in a later stage, only then it may manifest in the form of confrontations with another member of the group. In a group that I once led, it seemed that a member's conflict with my role as an authority figure had been resolved. A few sessions later, however, this member assumed a posture of authority vis-à-vis another member in an attempt to place herself above that member.

The knowledge that groups go through identifiable stages of development will help leaders develop a sense of order and expectation (predictability) about group process. A good parallel is the knowledge parents acquire about the stages of child development: it provides them with a general idea of what behavior they can expect from their children in early childhood and what is appropriate in adolescence. They know that the norms they establish for their 9-year-old will have to be adjusted or abandoned when the child reaches 15. Likewise, acquiring knowledge of the developmental processes for each stage of group therapy before they undertake to lead a group will help therapists avoid a good many difficulties and will facilitate the growth process.

An understanding of the stages of group development allows co-leaders to demystify the confusing and highly complex interactive dynamics of a group of diverse individuals. Agazarian and Peters (1981) cite other strong reasons for group therapists to be knowledgeable about group stages:

> This is why there is a significant difference between the therapy group whose therapist does individual therapy within the setting of a "group" of people, without the understanding of group development theory, and the therapy group whose therapist understands group process and employs group developmental theory. The group process therapist is able to influence deliberately the process of group development therapeutically at the same time that he deliberately chooses to influence individual development therapeutically; thus contributing both to the interdependence between the individual therapeutic potential and the potential for the group environment. The individually oriented therapist is not able to influence group development deliberately and will not have that choice until he has become familiar with group process as distinct from individual interests. (p. 128)

In our view, all three elements are affected by the developmental process of the group. We go into this at length in Part IV, where we discuss intervention, but let us note a few points here. The group is an interactive social system, and leaders need to be mindful that this system consists of *three* elements: leader, member, and the group as a whole. It is not just the group that is going through developmental stages; each of its members and its leader(s) are also. A fair analogy is the family: as the family as a whole goes through developmental stages, so do each of the other elements—the children and parents. It is also important to bear in mind that how each element manages the stage of development will affect the other two.

It is not realistic to expect each element to simultaneously arrive at or function at the same stage. (Again, a parallel can be found in family development, where each of the elements is at various stages of development.) This is a further reason for leaders to be acutely alert to developmental processes.

Group therapists need a conceptual framework of group development that suits their leadership style. As Kottler (1994) so aptly put it, "All researchers, theoreticians, and practitioners would agree that therapeutic groups progress through a series of stages, even if there is considerable disagreement as to how many stages there are and what they should be" (p. 42). Indeed, a review of the literature on theories of group development would leave one hard pressed to determine which theory is most valid. Typically, theories of group development are highly colored by the researcher's or the therapist's experience or point of view. Rogers (Donigian & Malnati, 1987), for example, identifies 15 stages through which groups pass. Yalom (1985), on the other hand, holds to a three-stage model.

Levine (1991) has identified several schools of thought regarding group development and has classified them according to type of groups. For instance, intensive group psychotherapists base their position on long-term therapy groups that focus on the

> emotional and/or depth of interpersonal growth or insight. There are sequential theorists. There are those who see group development as characterized by the recurrence of basic themes. Still others see group development based on the short-term training group approach. There are social group workers who base their theories on the supportive treatment and socialization groups with which they work. (pp. 65–67)

Levine concludes that there are essentially two classifications of group development, based on the duration of the group. *Long-term groups* are more likely to develop through a cyclical process, and *shorter-term groups* are more likely to develop along a sequential path. Among those who subscribe to the sequential-path view are Corey (1990), Gladding (1991), Jacobs,

Harvill, and Masson (1994), Napier and Gershenfeld (1993), Tuckman (1965), and Vanderkolk (1985).

Our own experience teaches us that groups develop through five sequential stages (Hansen, Warner, & Smith, 1980). In the initial stage, *orientation*, the leaders help to establish structure, norms, and goals and to build group culture. Their role resembles the role parents play in the formative period of the family. In Stage 2, *conflict*, the leaders help individual members work through such themes as dominance, control, and power. In Stage 3, *cohesiveness*, leaders strive to heal the bruises incurred in Stage 2, by facilitating member-to-member bonding and encouraging members to deal with matters related to intimacy.

The fourth stage of group development is analogous to what a family goes through as a child reaches later adolescence and early adulthood, when parents find they need to let go and allow their offspring to fend for themselves. In the group's life, this is referred to as the *work* stage. Leaders lower their profile and use the skills of listening, receiving feedback, and reframing old materials in ways that allow members to gain new perspectives about themselves. In the fifth and final stage, *termination*, leaders help members make the transition from the group to their other social environments.

The more leaders familiarize themselves with the developmental sequences that groups go through, the more likely they will be able to convey a mastery of group process. This, in turn, will help members entrust themselves to the leaders.

COHESION

Cohesion is generally defined as a sense of belonging or attraction to a group. Each element influences the other toward or away from group cohesion.

In general, the greater a member's feelings of attraction to or belongingness to the group, the more likely that member will be to feel his or her presence is vital to the group and the more likely that member will be to "risk" participating in and contributing to the group. For group cohesion to occur, *member behavior* must be elicited—that is, members must actively participate in talking about their concerns. Thus *leader behavior* requires interventions that stimulate members to talk. *Group behavior* often influences the degree to which members will talk about their concerns. For instance, a therapy group can manifest group behavior that is resistant to participating, that says: "*We* won't talk, or *we* are reluctant to talk at this time." Group behavior, in this case, is restricting the development of group cohesion.

To promote cohesion, leaders must encourage interactions. Often, to do this, they have to address group behavior instead of focusing on member behavior. For example, they may reassure the group as a whole that reluctance to participate is not unusual in beginning groups, or they may ask the group to examine its resistance to talking by saying "What makes it difficult for any new group to get started?"

As we said, each element influences the others to move toward or away from cohesion. At different junctures in group therapy, one element usually exerts more influence than the other two. However, to further the process of cohesion, each element must be able to interact freely with the others.

POWER VERSUS INFLUENCE

The group therapist who understands and learns how to use process has also learned how to manage the power of the group, and how the leader harnesses the power of group process will determine therapeutic outcomes. Note that we are *not* saying here that leaders have power. The power for change resides in the *group*. The leaders, through their expertise, knowledge of group processes, and leadership role in the group, have the *potential* to influence how the group evolves and functions.

We mentioned earlier that neophyte leaders often feel overpowered by the group. At such times, they are allowing their reactive motives to dominate them, so they resort to restrictive solutions. Often these take the form of authoritarian responses. Their anxiety has so overwhelmed them that they fail to see that the way out of this highly intense moment is to use their *influence*. As leaders increasingly realize that authority and power are not synonymous, they come to rely on their knowledge of group process to influence the group.

STRUCTURAL FACTORS

Choosing a Co-Therapist

Many writers agree that the quality of the relationship between co-therapists can strongly affect the course and outcome of therapy (Corey, 1990; Gladding, 1991; Levine, 1991; Roller & Nelson, 1993; Yalom, 1985). Choosing a co-therapist, then, is not a task to be taken lightly. One of the primary considerations is that the two of you be on an equal footing in every respect to allow for free dialogue, discourse, function, and behavior throughout your time together. Mutual respect is implied in this requirement. You need not have exactly the same style and philosophy, but it is essential that you be philosophically compatible. In fact, identical styles and opinions can actually impede members' growth. Co-therapists who have some differences of opinion can facilitate group growth, member development, and co-leader development (that is, enabling solutions).

Complementariness is also generally beneficial. While the jury is still out as to whether male/female or same-sex co-therapy teams are more effective, we have found that the former type of pairing has a certain intrinsic value (for example, for transference).

The benefits of working with a co-therapist are qualitative. Let us run through some of them in no particular order of importance.

First, there is the advantage of having a colleague with whom you can discuss how things went in a session. Being the group's sole leader can be a lonely responsibility; having a partner with whom to share perceptions, experiences, and thoughts is highly valuable. Second, there are occasionally harrowing moments during sessions—a mass group attack on the leader, for example, the sudden departure of a member, or the occurrence of transference. A co-therapist can be of invaluable help in addressing the process of such occurrences. Third, there is a certain advantage to working like a tag team—when one of you becomes intensively involved, the other can objectively attend to the process of the interaction and remain aware of the group as a whole.

As you continue to work together with many different groups, you will undoubtedly discover the fourth advantage of having a co-therapist—the knowledge, with almost a sixth sense, of where your partner is and is going. It is an uncanny moment when you and your co-therapist are so in tune that you can make the follow-through intervention that brings added value and meaning to the experience a member or the group is having. Such synchronization only develops over time, however; it may take years of working together before you notice it.

So far we have spoken only of the benefits of co-leadership for the therapists. Are there any benefits for members and the group itself? Some authors believe that witnessing a complementary and equal relationship between male and female therapists gives members a model of how such relationships can function. Others contend that transference issues are more effectively worked through when both sexes are represented on the co-therapy team. The influence—and experience—that two therapists can bring to bear on the group can be extremely valuable. Moreover, when two therapists are leading a group, it is less likely that the group will be able to override them and fall back on restrictive solutions. Another benefit is that the group can continue when one of the co-leaders falls ill or misses a session for some other reason.

There are, of course, some limitations to working with a co-therapist, and these are often the obverse of the strengths we just mentioned. For instance, when co-therapists do not have equal status, it can lead to lack of trust and respect for one or both by the members. A parallel concern is the potential for competition between co-leaders. More than once, we have observed trainees competing with each other to establish the most supportive relationships with members (that is, transference) or to make the most astute process-illumination and theme-identification types of interventions. We have observed how power struggles between student co-therapists and ineffective communication between them leads to confusion on the part of members. Just as children sense when their parents are not in synch with each other and learn to take advantage of the disharmony, so do members of therapy groups seek to exploit disharmony between co-therapists. Yalom (1985) refers to this member tactic as *splitting the co-therapists*.

All these disadvantages notwithstanding, we believe that the benefits of a co-therapy team that works well together are worth the risk.

Member Selection and Group Composition

What people leaders select to participate in their groups will depend largely on the group's purpose. Leaders, then, need to clearly state the goal(s) of the group before they begin to select its members. Once they have done that, they should consider who will benefit most from participating in the group. Yalom (1985) suggests that people who are highly motivated and who have interpersonal problems ranging from loneliness, inability to establish and maintain intimate relationships, inability to love, low self-worth, and fear of success benefit the most from group therapy. Other authors support these observations (Corey, 1990; Piper & McCallum, 1994; Salvendy, 1993).

Leaders planning to form a group also need to weed out during the selection process people who would benefit least from group therapy or who would most likely engage in counterproductive or inhibiting behaviors in group. In our experience, the people who distract most from the group process are those who crave being the center of attention, who cannot tolerate ambiguity, and who are unable to manage anxiety. It is Yalom's (1985) view that people who are brain damaged, paranoid, hypochondriacal, suicidal, deeply depressed, or currently in a deep emotional crisis are poor candidates for group membership and should be excluded.

As part of the screening process, therapists need to consider a potential member's readiness or desire to join the group. This raises the issue of whether groups should be composed of members who volunteer or who are assigned (by the courts, for example). Clearly, when people are forced into your group, it raises the specter that the group will be perceived as a circle of banishment and its members will be poorly motivated or even hostile. Yet the reality for therapists who work in outpatient clinics, residential institutions, and psychiatric hospitals is that members of their groups generally have no choice but to attend. The essential thing for therapists leading such groups to remember is they must establish an orientation and preparation process that is sensitive to this issue. In fact, allowing members to express at the initial sessions how it feels to be forced into group frequently leads to universalizing issues, finding the group's common theme, and thus beginning to address the disturbing motives that led to their current difficulties. If leaders can convince such members that participating in a therapy group can benefit them, the first step toward developing members' motivation to participate fully will have been taken.

Where participation is entirely voluntary, can we compose the "ideal group"? Yalom (1985) has made useful points that acknowledge the basic reality faced by practitioners. Group leaders generally accept the first seven or eight candidates whom they have screened and believe will most likely make good group members. They tend to use broad criteria, trying for a fair representation of men and women, a wide age range, and a good balance between less and more vocally active members. As Yalom emphasizes, the therapists' primary concern at the outset is to develop a group capable of cohesiveness. Therapists generally find that if they carefully select and prepare candidates, they do not need to be overly concerned about composing an "ideal group."

Simultaneous Therapy—Group and Individual

The terms *concurrent, conjoint,* and *combined* are used to describe a situation in which individual and group therapy are offered to the same person simultaneously. Yalom (1985) distinguishes among these terms as follows: *concurrent therapy* involves two different therapists, one for group work and the other for individual therapy; *conjoint therapy* involves the same therapist for group and individual work with all members; and *combined therapy* involves having the same therapist who leads the group also do individual therapy with some of the members. Porter (1994) views simultaneous therapy as having "its own indications, contraindications, mechanisms of action, developmental stages and technical requirements" (p. 314). Most writers agree that when the two types of therapy—group and individual—are synchronized and working well together, the effect can be far more powerful than that of either type of therapy done in isolation. Let us look at some of the advantages of the simultaneous use of group and individual therapy.

When offered together, individual and group therapy can complement each other. Intrapsychic and interpersonal issues that were generated in the group but are too intense for members to feel comfortable exploring in front of other members can be explored first safely in the individual therapy setting. Another advantage is that shy members usually feel safer expressing themselves to a therapist in privacy—at least at first. This experience builds their confidence so that they can become more self-expressive in group. For these reasons, simultaneous therapy helps prevent members from prematurely leaving the group. For the member, it is highly beneficial to progress from working through interpersonal issues in individual therapy, to practicing them in the group, to applying them in other social settings. For the therapist, simultaneous therapy offers the opportunity to observe a member in both contexts and to use the knowledge gained in the two settings to benefit the member.

Still, there are some pitfalls to the simultaneous use of group and individual therapy. For many authors (Kaplan & Saddock, 1993; Piper & McCallum, 1994; Porter, 1994; Rutan & Alonso, 1982; Salvendy, 1993; Yalom, 1985), the disadvantage of concurrent therapy—or working with two different therapists—is that the therapists will probably not be in communication with each other and therefore each will be ignorant of what the other is doing. In fact, the two therapists may be working at cross-purposes. Obviously, this situation can be countertherapeutic for the member—being caught between two experts whose views are in opposition may be overwhelming.

The other forms of simultaneous therapy also have disadvantages. With both conjoint and combined therapy, group members may decide to sit silently in group and not deal with issues until they meet with the therapist individually. There is also the matter of confidentiality. Material a member presents in individual therapy, if held secret, potentially robs the group of its therapeutic value and power. Therapists need to realize that if, by becoming the repositories of such secrets, they allow a member to circumvent the group, they are actually working against themselves as group leaders. Yalom (1985) suggests that this problem is compounded when there are co-therapists and some members see one therapist, while other members see the other therapist. On the other hand, therapists who refuse to withhold secrets disclosed in individual sessions from the group cannot expect members to feel secure about exploring intense emotional material in individual therapy.

Simultaneous therapy, as you can see, has some very complex properties. Porter (1994), who is a strong advocate of conjoint therapy, and Kaplan and Saddock (1993) feel that the tide is moving in the direction of offering individual and group psychotherapy together. Rutan and Alonso (1982) are for making group therapy the primary modality, with individual therapy as a supplement. Yalom (1985), on the other hand, suggests that group therapy is quite sufficient, provided members are carefully selected. Our position is the same as Yalom's. The complex and fragile nature of the dual relationship fostered by simultaneous therapy almost inevitably saddles each mode of therapy with countertherapeutic factors. Unless the therapist is reasonably certain these factors can be overcome, we feel that it is best to stick to one mode of therapy at a time.

Group Size

The consensus among many writers (Corey, 1990; Jacobs, Harvill, & Masson, 1994; Piper & McCallum, 1994; Salvendy, 1993; Yalom, 1985) is that group size should generally range from 5 to 12 members. Perhaps the ideal number is 8 or 9. When deciding upon the size of a group, therapists need to take into consideration such factors as member attrition; whether or not the group will be led by co-therapists; the need to keep the group small enough to allow individuals to work through their issues, but large enough for interactive processes to occur; the purpose of the group; the age range of its members; and the experience of the therapists.

The predominant theme across the literature is that for group therapy to be effective, the therapists need to ensure there is ample opportunity for the actualization of interactive processes. If the group is too small (fewer than five members), there is a very high probability that the full power of group therapy will not be released. On the other side of the coin, small groups encourage more in-depth individual and therapist-to-member work. If the group is too large (more than 12 members), the large-group effect will occur, but the opportunity for each member to do in-depth work will be lost.

We believe that in groups led by co-therapists, the ideal size is 8 or 9 members, with 10 or 11 as the outer limit. Since in every group the premature termination of one or two members should be anticipated, a number much lower than 8 would make the presence of two therapists an overly dominant factor, with detrimental effects on group interactiveness.

PART III

GROUP STAGES

While we acknowledged earlier in this book that groups can go through either sequential or cyclical stages of development, we have opted to present the sequential model in this part. The characteristics of the stages in both models of development are the same. The difference is that the sequential model is more apt for time-limited groups, and the cyclical model for time-extended and/or open groups.

INTRODUCTION

We have said that a therapy group is an evolving social system that goes through several stages of development. At each stage, the group has needs that must be met and characteristics that are peculiar to that moment in its life. Certain dynamics (actions/behaviors) also are symptomatic* of that period of development.

Much has been written about the stages of groups and many models have been proposed to reflect the life stages of a therapy group. Hansen, Warner, and Smith (1980), after doing a comprehensive review of the literature, suggested that groups go through five distinguishable stages of development: orientation, conflict and confrontation, cohesiveness, work, and termination. These are the stages we discuss in this part of the book. Agazarian and Peters (1981) not only identify stages of group development but also support our view that a therapy group is a unique social system with a complex interactional process.

When we refer to the group as a social system, we mean that it has the properties of a social system and therefore behaves like one. As you will recall, there are three elements that make up this system, and these elements are interdependent, so a change in one will have a subsequent effect upon the others. Furthermore, as a social system, the group attempts to maintain a state of equilibrium or homeostasis at each stage of its development. Growth from one stage to the next will occur only if the equilibrium is challenged or the homeostasis is disrupted. The inevitable consequence of such a challenge or disruption is the experience of discomfort in each of the elements. This discomfort (conflict) is potentially the engine of change. Therefore the tension or anxiety accompanying it is to be viewed by the leader as necessary for group movement. It is important that the group leader understand that at every developmental stage each element will manifest tension in a way that is peculiar to it. We encourage

---

* The symptomologies of each period of development manifest themselves in recognizable (identifiable) behaviors.

leaders to become accustomed to being uncomfortable and to learn to turn *toward* the discomfort. View discomfort not a foe, but as a friend of effective group therapy.

STAGE 1: ORIENTATION

Characteristics

Stage 1 is a multilevel stage. There are hidden agendas. Activity is at the subvocal (self-talk) and vocalized levels. There is an effort to establish goals and the means for achieving them. Group norms and codes of conduct are sought. There is also some disillusionment and confusion. Safe public images are presented, while personally relevant material is not. Eventually a new reality develops. The most dramatic manifestation of this new reality is the identification of a common object for fantasy projections. Often the leader is selected to receive these projections—though not solely. Out of this new reality develops permission for member-to-member confrontation. The emotional climate at the outset of Stage 1 is usually tense, awkward, and ambiguous. As the group approaches the terminus of this stage, the tension is of a different order—anticipatory of conflict, revolution, and resistance to moving forward and beyond.

Member Element

Individuals engage in a great deal of intrapsychic activity at this stage. For instance, they may ponder how to present themselves without appearing foolish to the others, or they may be concerned about whether or not they are attractive to the other members. Another popular covert activity takes the form of *psyching out* the other members. This is an attempt to anticipate the needs and wants of the others so that, by meeting them, a member might gain social acceptance and approval. Another way in which members seek acceptance is to engage in socially accepted codes of conduct.

Individuals are polite to one another at this stage; they tend to support and agree with each other. Problems are addressed rationally, devoid of any intense emotional tone. This is also the period when participants are establishing their position and/or role in the group. Projection and transference of family-of-origin material occur, leading to the reenactment of old (familiar) behavior patterns. For instance, in one group, Sam was observed to respond to Bonnie's reproach of Sylvia by moving to Sylvia's defense. This pattern of behavior repeated itself over the next two sessions. When the dynamics of this triadic interaction were illuminated to all three participants, they each disclosed how they had been affected by the other and how that led to their behaving as they did. Sam related that he was the oldest of four siblings, and that when Bonnie attacked Sylvia, he responded as he had when his next-oldest sibling attacked his youngest sibling—his intention was to even up the sides. Not surprisingly, Bonnie said that Sylvia's behavior reminded her of her younger sister, who received continual support from her parents as the *baby of the family.* Sylvia remarked that she was not consciously aware that her presenting style generated the kind of responses Sam and Bonnie were describing. However, she did relate that the way she habitually dealt with conflict in her family of origin was to engage in behaviors designed to diffuse anger and draw caretaking responses from her parents. She added that she felt a familiar (similar) anxiety grip her when she entered the group.

During this stage, members will attempt to resolve any social-relationship issues that arise. This is also the time when various concerns are identified, such as the members' search for meaning in life and their reason for joining the group. In general, the focus is less on the self and more on social interactions. Members fear rejection, and this fear often manifests itself in deprecation of the group (telling oneself it is not real and so forth). What members expect of one another and of themselves is brought into question. Self-exploration is not spontaneous. Self-description is often couched in the third person.

Group Element

At this time, group culture is developing and the group's rules of conduct are being established. Psychological and physical boundaries are blurred—that is, the group often seems to be in flight or fight. Individuals either retreat into themselves, or they express how they are not the same as (emphasize their differences from) the others. Primitive fears related to safety, rejection, and intimacy (sexual, emotional, psychological) are prevalent. There is no clear differentiation among members, so conformity prevails. Members may attack the leader—for example, by questioning the leader's competence. It almost seems a revolution is necessary if the group is to move beyond this point. (In fact, most therapy groups do not progress beyond this level.) The group struggles with ambivalent feelings about moving forward or remaining at the same place (to grow or not, to stay in the group or to leave).

Leader Element

Leaders bring their own pregroup histories to the group, especially their family-of-origin and nuclear-family experiences. Thus the possibility of countertransference is very real. Leaders at this stage are concerned to reduce group and individual projections (such as expectations to be hero/heroine). There are a number of other matters group leaders face in Stage 1. One is managing their own anxiety, which is generated by the group's and individual member's expression of feelings of disillusionment and confusion. As the leader struggles to avoid becoming the central character in the group—a struggle characterized by issues related to power, control, and authority—there is also the primitive fear of being rendered powerless, of being taken over or rejected by the group (which exists at least at a preconscious level). Therapists at this stage are trying to anticipate the expectations of the group, which requires them to deal with their own fantasies of the leadership role (for example, being a benevolent parent figure and/or a helpful caretaker). In addition, they confront the need to reconcile their idealized view of group leadership with their realistic view of it. For instance, they may think that the ideal leader is omniscient— or at least gives the appearance of being so.

At this stage, leaders need to decide how to enter the group and what level of involvement they should maintain. For example, some leaders try to enter the group more as a member than a leader in an effort to shrink members' perception of them as experts. The challenge then becomes one of maintaining this position while facilitating group process.

Managing the group's pace is another concern leaders face in Stage 1. The pace the group is moving at may be quite different from the leader's desired pace.

One student leader we knew, for example, worked diligently to maintain a group-centered position; he did not want to appear to be the expert. However, during a session early in the group's life, it seemed to him that the group was avoiding its task. The student leader broke out of his self-imposed low profile and chastised the members for not facing up to the task at hand. Considering the stage this group was at, the avoidance had some legitimacy. Even more significantly, the group was functioning at a pace that matched members' emotional readiness. The leader, feeling frustrated with what he perceived as the group's lack of desire to function at a deeper emotional level, chose to abandon his original position and become more central to the group. The effect upon the group was one of shock, since the members felt they were performing at an emotional level that was acceptable to all. Typical Stage 1 issues related to power, control, and authority were characteristic here: The leader had to deal with his own anxiety related to the group and individual members' feelings of disillusionment, confusion, and ambiguity, while struggling to minimize becoming the group's central character. The therapist failed to deal with his own fantasies regarding the leadership role—that he could both be "just one of the group" and drive the group along at the faster pace he favored. He needed to reconcile his idealized image of himself as a leader with a more realistic image.

❖ ❖ ❖

Sample questions to be asked at this stage by the leader regarding the Member Element:

At this initial stage, what can be expected from the members concerning the content level of discussion?

Why do the members seem to be discussing mostly matters that are intellectually and emotionally safe?

How realistic is it to expect the members to disclose intimate issues at this stage?

Why do each of the members seem to avoid first-person references?

What things do the members seem to fear most at this stage? Why?

❖ ❖ ❖

Sample questions to be asked at this stage by the leader regarding the Group Element:

Why does the group seem reluctant to stay focused on a single issue?

Why does the group appear to be so concerned about knowing the rules of conduct?

What explains the group's hyperconcern with issues regarding safety, trust, and intimacy?

Why is the group's pace of growth so slow?

❖ ❖ ❖

Sample questions to be asked at this stage by the leader regarding the Leader Element:

Why do I feel uncomfortable about assuming the leadership role?

Why am I so concerned about what expectations each member may have of me?

Why am I so worried about whether I can control this group? What am I afraid will happen if I lose control over the group?

Why can't I shake off the desire to take care of that quiet and soft-spoken member?

I would like to let this group know it is started, but why am I afraid to do so?

Stage 2: Conflict and Confrontation

Characteristics

The overall climate at this stage is one of conflict and confrontation. Issues are more complex than anticipated. Feelings of powerlessness are being manifested as frustration born of an inability to change behaviors of self or others. Boundary testing is very evident, especially in the area of intimacy. Dominance, control, and power are the usual themes. The leader can expect to be attacked by and to experience various forms of resistance from the group.

Member Element

At the outset of this stage, members generally reflect high anxiety. The struggle between maintaining autonomy and entrusting oneself to the group (and intimacy) produces conflict that often manifests in angry statements and resistance. Members show hostility toward one another, especially as their efforts to maintain their individuality continue. How much of oneself to reveal and how much difference from others will be tolerated are questions that arise out of the complexity attendant on becoming intimate. Some members emotionally disengage, others threaten to leave the group (in fact, some do), while still others become aggressive and go on the attack.

In one of our groups, Joe was not an active participant during the group's early sessions, when a number of the other members confronted one another and reached a common understanding. Joe continued to maintain an emotional distance until, finally, he was challenged for cutting himself off from emotional encounters and refusing to become a bona fide member of the group.

While this conflict concerned the intimacy boundary, other boundaries are also tested during Stage 2. For instance, individual significance may be challenged through "absence"—

presenting only good/best ideas, and then remaining silent. Authority is also challenged at this stage. Members will often attack the leader for incompetence, lack of emotional engagement, and the like. Old ways of coping with conflict are not functioning, so an individual member may acquiesce to group pressure and relinquish defense mechanisms habitually used to maintain autonomy.

Gradually, members engage in behaviors signaling the emergence of trust. People give up their efforts to maintain an ego-centered state as membership in the group becomes more attractive. Joe, for example, eventually dropped his reticence and engaged in behaviors that reflected trust of the group. His trust-reflecting behaviors included self-disclosure and transparency—which required him to take some risk. Such behaviors signaled his desire to be included in the group, which came about, in part, because of the leader's facilitation of group process.

During this stage, however, there is still an atmosphere of uncertainty. Since restrictive solutions to conflict are proving unreliable, members are challenged to discover enabling solutions to cope with the socialization process. Toward the end of this stage, members either become willing to accept cohesiveness as a viable alternative to the long period of intense discomfort engendered by conflict and confrontation, or they take flight and regress to safety. Thus this is a pivotal stage in the life of a therapy group.

Group Element

As the group moves from Stage 1 to Stage 2, tension pervades the membership. Various forms of intrapsychic energy surge to the surface in the form of raw emotion. This may take the form of loud expressions of anger (shouting), challenges of one another's maintenance of psychological and emotional safety (distance), and expressions of anxiety stemming from pressures related to intrapsychic conflict. Members admonish one another. Sometimes they set up double-bind* situations and establish a certain form of quid pro quo. The latter can manifest itself in subtle ways. For instance, members may subgroup into dyadic or triadic alignments designed to deal with mythical (archetypical) threats to survival. Unlikely partnerships are formed (I won't attack you, but instead will align myself with you in the hope that you will reciprocate). A "war" over issues of control, dominance, and power preoccupies the group.

Usually these themes manifest in the form of attacks on the leader(s) or the subject matter being addressed and/or a general avoidance of work. Such avoidance should be viewed as group resistance, though the resistance very often takes a passive form and therefore is not readily recognizable. Unless these matters are resolved at this stage, the group will likely remain at a superficial level, with invisible subgroup boundaries and the persistence of transference issues. It is important for the group to express and explore differences between and among members.

Leader Element

Leaders bring their own prehistory concerning conflict to this stage of group therapy, and unless they have truly come to terms with this prehistory and developed functional ways of addressing the conflicts and confrontations characteristic of this stage, the group will become mired in a morass of unresolved issues that will keep it from making an effective transition to Stage 3. The risk of countertransference is especially high if the leaders have not managed to put to rest their own ghosts of past conflictual situations. The following example illustrates how countertransference might be manifested in Stage 2.

---

*A double-bind situation is one in which, no matter what the individual does, he or she is chastised for it. For example, a person may be criticized for maintaining emotional distance; then, when he or she expresses strong feelings, these may be rejected as inappropriate. A double bind is a no-win situation.

A group one of our students was co-leading was struggling with issues of psychological and emotional intimacy. This struggle took the form of heated exchanges between and among members. The student leader's response to the emotional intensity generated by these encounters was to remain silent for a while, and then move to terminate the session by engaging in parenting-type responses that ignored the conflictual issues. Later, during postgroup supervision, the leader said she had been aware of the intensity of the group's encounter, but had not realized how she had opted to deal with it. Upon reflection, she owned that what she had done during the group's conflict was to take on the role she used to assume whenever members of her family of origin would fight—that of placating or pacifying the others.

The following week the group engaged in emotionally safe and intellectually light discussion. The leader's postgroup supervision session of the previous week helped her to recognize that the group was avoiding the unresolved issues from the week before. Armed with self-awareness regarding her restrictive approach to coping with conflict that week, she acknowledged her nonfacilitative response in the preceding session, and then led the group to face their unresolved issues. Thus this therapist prevented the continuation of a norm that would have had the group spinning its emotional wheels.

The anxiety leaders tend to experience at Stage 2 is usually related to the intrapsychic conflict—the internal civil war—that results when they revert to old forms of addressing challenge(s) the group and members are confronting them with, even though they know the situation demands a different response. Often at this juncture leaders choose to disregard the more emotional means of responding, opting to be guided instead by rational and cognitive means that satisfy their safety needs. In doing so, they may unwittingly establish norms that prevent the group from growing. For instance, the leader's behavior may indicate that it is okay for the group and/or individual members to talk about anger, but the expression of angry feelings will not be tolerated. Moreover, leaders who opt for a more intellectual and safe intervention convey to the group the message that they cannot be relied upon to manage the risky entry into emotion-laden issues that reflect members' need to express and explore their uniqueness (differences). The result is that individual members and the group as a whole are insulated from conflictual or toxic issues.

Sample questions to be asked at this stage by the leader regarding the Member Element:

Why do the members seem to be overly anxious?

Why are the members expressing such hostility toward one another?

Why does a certain member seem to have withdrawn emotionally from the group at this time?

Uh-oh, why didn't I hear from the member who is absent tonight?

Wow! Why are they challenging me?

Why do so many of the members seem so unsure of themselves?

Sample questions to be asked at this stage by the leader regarding the Group Element:

What makes this group seem so tight (tense)?

They are so vehement in expressing their anger—what is causing that vehemence?

There seems to be an unholy alliance among those three—why are they relating to one another so closely?

Why is it that most of the toxic issues are over power and control?

All they seem to do is get angry with one another. Why is no one willing to work through anything?

Sample questions to be asked at this stage by the leader regarding the Leader Element:

Why am I feeling so threatened by the aggressive and angry expressions of emotions that are occurring in the group?

I feel that person who is attacking me is just like my father. Why do I want to respond as I do?

I really feel torn. One part of me wants to bring this group to a more rational level, but another part of me feels I ought not to distract the group from these feelings. Why do I feel this way?

My mother and father used to fight like that, and right now I feel as I did back then in my family—I'd like to go and hide. What should I do?

STAGE 3: COHESIVENESS

Characteristics

What distinguishes this stage from the preceding two is a marked change in the emotional tone of the group. It is the calm after the storm. Boundary lines are not as rigid: individuals are permitted to maintain their personal boundaries and still be included in the group without being challenged. The group now allows for emotional closeness. The tasks at this stage are to heal the bruises from the previous stage and to bond. There is an emotional cohesion in the group at this point.*

Member Element

Members are decidedly different at this stage. They are willing—even eager—to be self-disclosing. Individuals tend to drop their false fronts (facades) and members perceive one another as more genuine. This movement toward honesty breeds an emotional and psychological intimacy (closeness) that is strongly cohesive. Individual differences are now downplayed; members discover previously unrealized similarities among themselves. Often one member will say to another "I identify with you."

The leader and the group itself become objects of identification for the members. Group participants develop a commitment to one another. During this stage, members who have demonstrated a greater sense of self-comfort and who seem to be more psychologically and emotionally centered

*Slavson (1957) cautions therapists to be on the lookout for the *pseudo*cohesiveness and *pseudo*intimacy that can occur in this stage. Generally, this false cohesiveness or false intimacy is recognizable by the almost saccharine nature of the bonding behavior members engage in. What has happened is that the group inaccurately believes it has resolved the conflicts generated in Stage 2, when, in reality, it has prematurely disengaged from that stage. Thus the group has the false impression that it has survived conflicts and confrontations, its work is now done, and the members can rejoice.

than the others usually gain influence in the group. They evolve into positions of authority, perhaps even assuming leadership roles. Other members will take on roles reflecting the function they have served in the group (for example, nurturer, sacrificer, mediator) and held in their family of origin.

Other behavioral indices of this stage are: members arrive on time, absenteeism is virtually nonexistent, individuals do not leave the group, and members state that they look forward to sessions. There is a universality about members' feelings regarding the group. Still, it will be apparent at this stage that one or two members have not joined the group emotionally; they continue to engage in intellectually safe interchanges. Often they are perceived as the slowest members of the group, and other members will make concerted efforts to include them in the group. Indeed, these slower participants frequently say they still feel like outsiders. Such admissions have a seductive quality and draw a great deal of energy from the other members as they try to enfold these "outsiders" into the group.

Group Element

In contrast to the situation in the first two stages, the group now has a sense of direction. Partly this comes from the fact that members are making a greater effort to adhere to the group's norms; this self-regulation makes the need for constant overt policing unnecessary.

At this point, the group seems an entity—a unique social system with its own norms and internal arrangements. A certain level of intimacy prevails, making possible the exploration of psychological and emotional closeness between and among members. Sexual intimacy is an ever-present danger at this stage, for there is often an erotic quality to the intimacy. Sexual intimacy could lead to subgrouping that would destroy the facilitative quality of the group. Still, for the most part, the group reflects a unified social system, evidenced by an increase in group morale and mutual trust.

Leader Element

The danger for leaders at this stage is they may accept Stage 3 as the terminus of the group's life when it is in reality the group's midpoint. Because the previous stage was characterized by strong affect and was experienced by members and leaders alike as emotionally draining, the emotional calm and unified appearance of the group in Stage 3 will be a welcome respite.

The leader's role will change at this point, requiring less visibility. The shift to a lower profile may prove difficult at first, but letting go of the group and allowing it to assume responsibility for its direction can be a stimulating challenge instead of a threat. Leaders need to remember that this is precisely what they were working toward, even though the greater independence of the group may raise doubts in their minds as to their own value and role. Entrusting more control to the group tends to create difficulties when leaders have not resolved their own anxiety about letting go.

Leaders need not fear inactivity or less responsibility at this stage, for they will still have to attend to group process carefully. They must also be alert to the temptation to believe that the level of intimacy the group has achieved is the terminal stage. If they believe this, the group will surely resist moving to Stage 4, where deeper levels of self-exploration will occur. Leaders must fight their own inclination to avoid the possibly uncomfortable work of the next stage. They will need to confront members regarding their need to pursue self-exploration to a greater depth. As they do so, their behavior may surprise members because it will be so different from their earlier behavior supporting the group's movement toward cohesiveness. Challenging the group's avoidance of responsibility for deeper levels of work may make leaders temporarily unpopular, but this is an absolutely necessary leadership task at this stage of the group's life.

❖ ❖ ❖

Sample questions to be asked at this stage by the leader regarding the Member Element:

Why does it seem that each member is finding that he or she can identify with other members more now than at earlier stages in the group's life?

Why do the members no longer personalize the challenges they issue to one another?

Why is the rest of the group spending so much time on those two members who have frequently expressed how unlike the others they are?

❖ ❖ ❖

Sample questions to be asked at this stage by the leader regarding the Group Element:

What is going on here? Members seem to be almost too sugar-sweet with one another.

Why am I feeling so anxious about confronting members about the need to spend more time addressing their personal issues?

Is it usual to experience a group as being this close psychologically and emotionally?

The group seems less concerned about rules and is setting its own direction—what has happened here?

How far do I allow these two members to go? They seem to be taking intimacy beyond the usual psychological and emotional bonding to the sexual area.

Sample questions to be asked at this stage by the leader regarding the Leader Element:

This group has been through a great deal. Now that it is so together, does it really need to continue?

I have worked very hard to bring this group together, and they seem so close at this point. Do they really need me anymore?

Why do they continue to ignore me every time I try to help them move to a deeper level by asking them to explore their issues more fully?

Stage 4: Work

Characteristics

It is not easy to describe this stage because it is such an ambiguous (amorphous) one in the sense that it displays many of the characteristics of the previous three stages at different moments of its life. Owing to the higher levels of intimacy now characteristic of the group, the threat to individual autonomy surfaces (that is, members wonder how much to keep to themselves and how much to let go). Members may also chafe at the responsibilities they have incurred by joining in this new "family." Some members may actually choose to remain in Stage 3.

Generally, the emotional climate is more intense in Stage 4 than it was in Stage 3. This increase in emotionality may be attributed to the group's working through personally relevant issues as opposed to skating across the surface of their lives. This is not a hostile period, however. Unlike in Stage 2, confrontation is more likely to come in the form of feedback; it is not a probing or psychologizing process. The group remains in the here-and-now; the content is not new. Most members come to work, and do so—at least in the first few minutes of the session. The key to this stage is that the overall emotional level of group functioning is *deeper* than at any other period and members are making an effort to work through their emotional issues. After a particularly hard-work session, it is common for members to come to the next session exhausted and prone to avoid work.

Member Element

Generally, the qualities that individual members display at this time are more openness and flexibility and less defensiveness. Some individuals will increasingly rise to the challenge of self-exploration, while others will hold back. Members at this stage tend to objectify rather than personalize feedback, both as givers and receivers. They also attempt to modify their behaviors based on the feedback they have received. This means individual members will risk experimenting with new behaviors, and often gain new insights in the process. As a result of this greater *intrapersonal* (versus interpersonal) exploration, intimacy may reach an even deeper level.

Group Element

Member-to-member boundaries are less rigidly defined, and with this greater openness, cohesiveness increases so that the group is able to support deeper levels of (individual) exploration and encourage greater self-awareness. This often leads to insight and group support of individuals who act upon their newfound self-knowledge.

Group structure has a more functional purpose at Stage 4. Norms are now perceived as useful, but they are not maintained for their own sake. Attitudes and behavior patterns often occur simultaneously, with real emotional intensity setting off a form of emotional contagion. (Recall our earlier example of the member who propelled himself out of his chair toward the woman who had just disclosed her sense of "emptiness" and the rest of the group's response to the depth of her disclosure.) As the meaning of intimacy is explored in greater depth, the group develops a deeper emotional bond. It presses to maintain the strong relationships that have been achieved.

The group's cohesiveness at this stage facilitates a greater tolerance for criticism, for by now, members generally feel safe and trusting within the group. There is a spirit of "one for all, and all for one" permeating the group.

This can make moving to the next stage, which is termination, quite stressful. The group will commonly express the desire to continue as a group. As the group nears the end of Stage 4, it may also engage in moments of levity as a means of coping with the anxiety members feel as Stage 5, termination, looms.

Leader Element

Stage 4 can be a period of ambivalence for leaders. The group now has its own motivation, and leaders may find it difficult to maintain a low profile and allow the group its lead. Yet maintaining a low profile may well be the most facilitative act in which the leader can engage.

At this stage, the need to use the finite skills of listening, confrontation in the form of feedback, and reframing old material so members can gain new perspectives on themselves can test a leader's own feelings of competency. A parallel to this experience is that stage of the parenting process when letting go of children as they reach later adolescence and assume more responsibility for their actions can be quite emotionally taxing for parents—especially when the children (members) are not engaging in and resolving personal matters as the parents (therapist) might. Leaders have to check their tendency to share their insights and experience with members too overbearingly lest they undermine members' hard-won maturity and independence. At the end of this stage, leaders will observe members moving toward integrating the self-knowledge they have gained in group in a way that will ultimately lead them to individuate from the group.

Sample questions to be asked at this stage by the leader regarding the Member Element:

Why do individual members not seem to be in a hurry to get through their own self-exploration?

Why is the feedback process no longer personalized?

Why have I not seen members trying to act on their feedback before?

Sample questions to be asked at this stage by the leader regarding the Group Element:

The group seems more willing to plunge into in-depth self-exploration than it was earlier. Why is that happening now?

The group seems much more flexible now and less concerned about what is the right and wrong thing to do. What has brought about this change?

Why is the group obviously not in a hurry to terminate? Why does it seem to want to continue?

Sample questions to be asked at this stage by the leader regarding the Leader Element:

Why do I feel somewhat at a loss about what to do now? The group seems to be doing fine without me.

Dare I risk pointing out that the pattern of interaction I am witnessing between those two members resembles the pattern they have reported employing in their family of origin?

Why do I find it so hard to allow the group simply to do its work without my being as visible as I was before?

STAGE 5: TERMINATION

Characteristics

There is an awkwardness about this last stage in the life of the group. Everyone, including the leader, is apprehensive about ending the group, and this apprehension will elicit all types of personal ways of dealing with endings, loss, separation, and aloneness. The overall emotional climate of the group will range from sadness to euphoria. Generally, matters that once kept certain members distanced from one another will no longer be barriers.

Member Element

Each member will display different coping behavior(s) related to endings. The existential issue of loss—the knowledge that this particular social system will be impossible to re-create ever again—will produce unique tensions in each person. In coping with this knowledge, members may draw upon coping mechanisms they used in their families of origin—in fact, the recapitulation of family losses may indeed be pertinent. Some members will want to move quickly to bring the process to a fast ending; others will want to delay the inevitable; still others who have invested less of themselves in the group will attempt to address unfinished business. Over the process hangs the threat that members may be unable to transfer the skills and knowledge they acquired through the group experience to other social settings. Thus the fear of being alone forever after the group disbands may haunt some members.

Group Element

Overall group interaction is relatively high in Stage 5. Everyone seems to have something to say, and there is a tendency to rehash the most significant events that each member experienced.* The group's pace may be hastened somewhat in anticipation of the impending termination, which runs the risk the group will move into denial. To diminish the effects of termination, members may exchange telephone numbers, agree to hold reunions, or meet at a local establishment immediately after the last group session. It is likely that the group will move into denial if anguish over termination is too great.

Leader Element

For leaders who have never adequately confronted their own existential issues concerning endings, Stage 5 can prove very difficult. One danger is that the leader will terminate the group prematurely, without helping it work through its existential angst about endings. Another danger is that the leader will attempt to delay or postpone termination and try to do unrealistic work for this period in the group's life (evidenced by asking the group if it has any unfinished business to address).

It is especially difficult for leaders to terminate a group that has been particularly close and has worked hard. Conversely, it is tempting for leaders to prematurely terminate a group that has proved especially difficult to work with. Overall, the leader's task at this stage is to regard Stage 5 as being as significant as all of the other stages in the group's life and to bring about closure in such a way that members can make the transition from the group to their other social environments effectively. To this end, leaders may want to share with the group the effect termination is having on them and explore how members might carry forward the transactions that have occurred within the life of the group.

*Acknowledgments of personal experiences and accomplishments and use of first-person references are quite common.

❖ ❖ ❖

Sample questions to be asked at this stage by the leader regarding the Member Element:

Why do those two members seem so intent on building a bridge between themselves at this late date?

Why is this member all of a sudden so self-disclosing? Where was this person earlier in the group?

Each of the members seems to be expressing different levels of feelings tonight—this is so different from our most recent session. Why is this happening?

I notice that those three really seem frightened that they might not be able to cope with their other social groups. Why does this seem to be such an issue when it was not one before?

❖ ❖ ❖

Sample questions to be asked at this stage by the leader regarding the Group Element:

I have never seen such a full range of emotions being displayed so openly. Why is this so?

Last week they did not seem to want to end the group, while tonight they act as though they cannot wait for it to end. What is causing this change?

Why are they all reminiscing about past sessions and talking about how good they feel now?

Why is that person passing out a map with directions to his house?

❖ ❖ ❖

Sample questions to be asked at this stage by the leader regarding the Leader Element:

Why do I feel so uneasy about the way the group is behaving?

How do I keep them from ending this session so soon?

How do I get them to see that we are ending and that maybe we ought to deal with endings?

I wonder if it will help if I disclose how I am feeling about our ending?

PART IV

INTERVENTIONS

Many new group therapists find it very difficult to conceptualize interventions and to decide which one(s) to apply in a given situation. We address the dimension of intervention in the following sections with the intention of whetting your appetite for the subject so that you will proceed to explore alternative interventions available to you, for our list is by no means exhaustive.

We conclude this section by discussing the blocks that inhibit effective intervention in the hope that if you thoroughly understand what these are, you will be able to free yourself of them.

PROCESS OF
CONCEPTUALIZING INTERVENTIONS

How to Decide Which Intervention to Employ

Always keep in mind that the whole purpose for using a group approach to therapy is to release the power of the group. This is where the therapeutic value of this type of therapy lies. Thus the most anxiety-provoking dimension of leading a therapy group for new leaders is conceptualizing interventions and deciding which ones will lead to releasing the power of the group. Therapists' anxiety can be traced to their own disturbing motives—the desire to avoid doing irrevocable harm to someone, the fear of being overpowered by the group, the desire to be liked, the need to be seen as a caring person. Such disturbing motives inevitably clash with reactive motives, which leads to restrictive solutions. Ultimately, this can develop into a spiraling process of continual counterproductive interventions based upon reactive motives.

One of the ways we have learned to avoid this spiraling process is to remind ourselves that to choose to do nothing is actually to opt for a restrictive solution—which will have consequences in the form of member and/or group responses. Armed with the awareness that we have to intervene with or manage various moments in the group, we have determined that it is necessary to approach the process of conceptualizing and choosing interventions by becoming aware of our own disturbing motives. If we learn not to deny their existence, they will eventually become old and familiar feelings, and as a result, we will be freed to more readily think in terms of a group process orientation.

Recall that we defined *group process* as the interactive relationship among the three elements: leader, member, and group. Our task as group leaders is to focus on *how* these elements interact with one another and to learn *why* they are doing so. Yalom (1985) refers to this task as listening and attempting to understand the "metacommunication" between the "actors." He uses as an example the student who raised his hand during a lecture on Freud and asked the lecturer the date of Freud's death. The lecturer's reply was "1938." To which the student inquired, "But sir, wasn't it 1939?" (p. 137).

Leaders who cue in on the *process* of this interaction can see that it contains a number of different levels and messages, any of which are fair game for leader intervention. For instance, "Why did this person ask a question he already knew the answer to?" "How did this person's response to the lecturer affect the other members of the audience (group)? The audience (group) as a whole?" "How has this person's response affected his role or position with other members and the group as a whole—now and for the future?" "How did the lecturer's response affect his role in the group?" "Might the lecturer have handled the student's inquiry differently?" For instance, suppose the lecturer decided to engage the other students in the interaction. Or suppose the lecturer chose not to address the content of the student's question but the process instead. In that case, the lecturer might have said, "It sounds to me as if knowing the date of Freud's death is important to you. What makes it so?" The point is, the assumptions that can be drawn from the process of the transaction between the "leader-lecturer" and the "group member-student" could take the level of their interaction—and that of other members and the group as a whole—to a deeper, more meaningful level.

Along with attending to the process of member, leader, and group interaction, there are a number of other factors we need to consider when conceptualizing and deciding on interventions. Among these are the anticipated or desired consequence that our intervention might have, the group's systems of communication, its history, themes, norms, and stage of development. Yalom (1985) feels that the needs of the group should be the primary determinants of leaders' choice of intervention. However, we believe that it is most important for leaders to consider how their intervention can best lead to releasing the group's power, for that is the purpose of doing therapy in a group format.

One final consideration is in order before we move on to discuss various types of interventions. New group leaders frequently try to anticipate too precisely what the group's or a member's response to an intervention will be. This can be inhibiting—if leaders feel they cannot anticipate exactly the consequence of their interventions, they may decide to make no intervention at all. We suggest that it is better to have something to deal with than nothing. Thus, if an anticipated consequence that does take place. (Every intervention has a consequence; no reaction, or silence, on the part of a member or the group is a consequence.)

With these considerations in mind, let us now consider the many types of interventions that are available to leaders.

TYPES OF AVAILABLE INTERVENTIONS

Co-Leader to Co-Leader

Among the least used and most underestimated of interventions is co-leader-to-co-leader communication. Too frequently co-leaders overlook the value of openly dialoguing with each other in front of members and the group as a whole. One value of this type of intervention is that open exchanges between co-leaders encourage open exchanges among group members (Bernard & MacKenzie, 1994). We also believe that open discussion and sharing of thoughts, feelings, and observations reassure members that co-leaders do not have hidden agendas concerning them.

Moreover, making members privy to co-leaders' motivations and collaborative efforts can lead to their gaining insight or self-awareness. For instance, because she believed in the value of sharing her process observation of the group as a whole with her co-leader, Sue was able to say, "Dan, I've got this feeling that what we're asking the group to do may be just too hard for them to face head-on. Perhaps we might be better off if we asked them what it is about this issue that makes it so hard to face directly." This kind of transaction between co-leaders is akin to that between two parents who know their kids are at the top of the stairs listening in on their conversation. The effect is powerful. The kids will get the message without being confronted head-on, so the chances of raising their defenses are minimized. By using this indirect route for communicating with the group as a whole, Sue was able to apprise Dan of her thoughts, and, through their metacommunication, he understood what her motives were. The message the group heard was that the leaders were acknowledging that it was a struggle for it to face an anxiety-provoking issue and, simultaneously, that the leaders were not chastising it for not addressing this difficult issue straightforwardly. The group was thus freed to address its *block* to approaching the fear rather than the fear itself. This intervention parallels what Yalom (1985) refers to as *using the subjunctive tense*. A safe and emotionally distant triangulated interaction occurred between each of the co-leaders and between the leaders and the group as a whole. This allowed the group to have a safe, once-removed experience.

Leader to Member

This is the intervention new leaders seem to find easiest to use. Perhaps the ease is born of the fact that therapists' earliest training is in individual therapy and that is therefore the therapy with which they are most familiar and feel most secure. The danger is that leaders who lean on this familiar type of intervention can be diverted into conducting individual therapy in a group format, thus losing the values of interactive group therapy.

We are by no means discouraging leader-to-member interventions. In fact, we see this type of intervention as highly valuable—so long as therapists remember when they use it that it is not affecting just one particular member but the entire system as well (that is, all three of the elements of group therapy).

Leader-to-member interventions are generally more pronounced during the first and second stages in the life of the group, when the leader is attempting to build a group culture and establish norms, as well as to model facilitative ways of interacting. Horwitz (1993) believes that by using an individualized approach, the therapist can eventually introduce the common theme that connects members of the group and thereby identify the common group tension. By listening with a "fourth ear," the therapist becomes consciously aware of group process and therefore can attempt to discover the underlying group theme. When incorporated in this manner, leader-to-member interventions are less likely to become individual therapy.

This concept was illustrated earlier in the case of Frank. As the therapist worked with him individually on his fear of living alone, she was able to identify themes of abandonment and mortality, which she then brought to the group's attention. The unveiling of this common theme (disturbing motive) of fearing to ultimately live and die alone gave the group permission to talk about it, and thus a common group tension was relieved.

Leader to Two or More Members

Certainly one of the values of group therapy over individual therapy is that the group is a social microcosm. Therefore interactions among and between its elements reflect what occurs in larger social systems. When two or more members are engaged in direct interaction with each other, then, the nature of their involvement (encounter) may be viewed as characteristic of each person's way of behaving in other social settings. When leaders observe these transactions, they can turn them into useful therapeutic interventions.

Most member-to-member interactions concern disturbing motives related to such themes as intimacy, autonomy, inclusion, powerlessness, and acceptance. With this in mind, it is the leaders' responsibility to address the *process* of these interactions rather than their content so that the experience becomes one from which the interacting members can learn.

New leaders, however, frequently succumb to the temptation to pay attention to the content of member-to-member interaction. It demands great discipline to listen to and understand the metacommunication of such transactions, to understand the *how* and *why* of them. As therapists gain experience, they learn that they do not have to focus on and recall every transaction and that it is okay to offer selective observations. Recall the moment when Sam, Bonnie, and Sylvia learned they were reenacting family-of-origin patterns of behavior. The co-leaders observed that the process of Sam's moving to Sylvia's defense had repeated itself over the past three sessions. As a result of the co-leaders' process illumination, all three members were able to express how they felt, to identify the source of their behaviors, to become self-empowered as a result of what they learned about themselves.

Leader to Subgroup

Subgrouping occurs in all walks of life. We find it in families, we see it in the workplace, in social gatherings, and in therapy groups. In other words, subgrouping is a normal phenomenon and should be expected by leaders. It is the function that subgrouping plays and its subsequent effect upon the group that is often called into question.

Bernard (1994), MacKenzie (1994), and Yalom (1985) agree that subgrouping can have a potentially inhibiting effect on the group. When two or more members agree to keep some matters confidential among themselves, when secrets are withheld from the group, when boundaries are violated and unfinished business from a session is concluded in private, alliances and coalitions are being formed that can subvert the group process. For this reason, leaders often discourage members from subgrouping. Yalom (1985), however, suggests that not all subgrouping is deleterious to groups. There are, in fact, times when what is discussed in private between two members outside of group can instigate the raising of an important issue or topic in group. We have frequently heard one member proclaim to another in group, "You know, I've seen you have no trouble talking when we meet out in the parking lot or when we've gone for coffee with others. I don't understand why you're having so much trouble talking up in the group." This open invitation for a fellow member to verbalize in front of the group an issue that is clearly of concern to that member has facilitative value and does not detract from the group's goals.

It is the task of the leaders to discern when member subgrouping has the potential for distracting the group from its goals. Attending to *how* and *why* two or more members have been meeting outside of group can be fruitful. Process-oriented leaders avoid restrictive solutions and instead engage in solutions that enable members to feel safe enough to address the disturbing motives that led to their extragroup socializing. So if leaders observe metacommunication or other forms of nonverbal communication between members that suggests they are subgrouping, they have the responsibility to the group as a whole and to the other members to address the matter. Subgrouping is generally a poorly kept secret anyway, so by bringing it into the open, the leaders will be giving the group permission to address it. Such moments afford leaders the opportunity to identify themes and move the group from a certain content focus to broader issues.

Leader to the Group as a Whole

"The purpose of a mass group interpretation is to remove some obstacle that has arisen to obstruct the progress of the entire group" (Yalom, 1985, p. 187). This statement implies that group-as-a-whole interventions need to be used carefully and discreetly. It also suggests how important it is for leaders to be sensitive to group process.

For example, in a session following one characterized by intense emotional encounters, the group as a whole was engaging in light conversation and gingerly avoiding matters of deep emotional concern. Taking note of this, the co-leaders offered the following process observation to the group: "You know, last week we were engaged in some pretty heavy stuff. Tonight you all seem to be walking on eggshells. Is there something going on that needs to be addressed?" By thus noting that the group's behavior this night was noticeably different from its behavior the preceding week, but without chastising the group in any way, the co-leaders offered empathy and invited the group to talk about whatever was inhibiting it from addressing matters of an emotionally deeper and more personal nature. Here again, the leaders were giving members the opportunity to present their disturbing motives. The group culture was such that the leaders protected members' feelings of vulnerability while encouraging risk-taking behavior.

Leader Self-Disclosure

There are many arguments for and against leader self-disclosure. Yalom (1985) contends that therapist self-disclosure can establish a model of self-disclosure for members. Weiner (1993), on the other hand, cautions leaders to be very careful about self-disclosures that go beyond their professional training. It is our position that when members request of leaders personal disclosures, leaders should attempt to discern *why* the request is being made and what value a full disclosure will have for the group as a whole. Very rarely do group members seek knowledge of leaders without an underlying disturbing motive. Even so, leaders need to be careful not to sound evasive or appear emotionally aloof. When presented with such a moment, a leader may respond by saying something like "I am willing to answer your request, but it would be helpful for me to know how my answer will help you." In this way, the leader encourages the member to disclose his or her disturbing motive while simultaneously setting the stage for a safe interchange (enabling solution).

There are times, especially in the early stages in the group's life, when leaders can use self-disclosure to help build norms and group culture. During these stages, members often engage in behaviors that are counterproductive and inhibit group movement. By focusing the self-disclosure on the effect a member's behavior or that of the group as a whole is having upon the therapist, the therapist models how to express feelings (fears, hurt, disappointment, anger, affection, and the like). In addition the leader is introducing the idea that the members and the group as a whole are ready to tolerate increasing levels of intimacy.

Member to Member

Encouraging member-to-member interaction is one of the more important functions of group therapists. This type of intervention is usually most acute in the first stage of the group's life. At that time, member behavior is inclined to be less interactive. Verbal expressions are likely to be in the third-person there-and-then, since members are reluctant to address one another directly. Either a member will talk about another member to the group or will attempt to talk about the other member indirectly by talking directly to the therapist. The motives behind such behavior are many, but generally it can be ascribed to anxious feelings generated by fears of rejection, intimacy, inadequacy, and conflict.

Such interventions are quite natural, so leaders should expect them. They also need to see such interventions as an opportunity to establish norms and build a group culture. By encouraging members to address each other directly and in the first person, leaders not only enable members to air their disturbing motives but also establish norms of speaking in the here-and-now and the first person and discourage talking through the leader(s). Support of direct speech in member-to-member interaction increases the potential for member bonding.

In a group that one of our student leaders was co-leading, a rather heated exchange between two members led to one of the members verbally attacking the other, who then began to cry. Before the leader could address the moment, a third member turned to her and said, "I don't think what Cindy said to Suzanne was fair!" Faced with a number of possible interventions to choose from, the leader opted to say, "Joyce, it sounds like you were quite affected by the way Cindy interacted just now with Suzanne. Why don't you tell her that directly and also tell her what it was about the way she treated Suzanne that has you feeling as you do." By encouraging Joyce to deal with Cindy directly, the leader was reinforcing member-to-member versus member-through-leader-to-member interaction (that is, leader-centered interaction). She also supported self-disclosure of a disturbing motive and the employment of an enabling solution. Thus the leader advanced the group's culture as one in which conflict and confrontation would be tolerated and emotional and psychological intimacy would be fostered, toward the end of member bonding.

Mentioning the Unmentionable*

In the children's fable "The Emperor's New Clothes," an Emperor regularly held a parade so that he could show off his stylishly extravagant new clothes. Finally, his tailors lost their creative edge and could not think up a radical new suit design that would please him. Out of fear of losing their heads for failing the Emperor, they informed him that they had just made him a suit from a magical material that was invisible to his eyes, but would be visible to the grosser eyes of his subjects. As the Emperor proceeded to march in the parade to show off his new clothes, the populace saw that he hadn't a stitch on him, but feared to say so. Instead, they applauded him, as they had done hundreds of times before. The exception was a young child, who exclaimed, "But Mother, he is not wearing any clothes!" After hearing the child's words, the Emperor realized he had been made a fool of, and quickly dispatched his tailor's heads. Perhaps it is this fear of being dispatched by a member or the group as a whole that inhibits leaders from mentioning the unmentionable. Yet it is essential for leaders to overcome their own disturbing motives so they can help a member or the group overcome their blocks to growth.

During the early stages of the group, member-to-member interaction generally remains at intellectually safe levels. Topics that would reveal disturbing motives are avoided, and the group as a whole is less likely to address such matters directly. This is understandable and can be expected (we refer you back to Part III, Group Stages). However, there will come a time in the group's life when the members and the group itself need to be encouraged to face those underlying fears that they dread will lead to a catastrophic consequence.

*Also see "Confrontation" on page 98.

Both elements need to see that the revelation of such fears will be tolerated. At such times as these, leaders need to demonstrate how members can verbalize seemingly intolerable topics. They need to uncover the fears that members have avoided facing, and to do so in such a way that members will see that they, the leaders, will tolerate both them and the consequences of mentioning the unmentionable. Of course, leaders should be sure that such revelations will be at a level that they feel secure in managing.

Certainly the timing of this type of intervention is important. Leaders need to remember that while they may be quite capable of managing some emotionally toxic issues, individual members and the group may not, since they have not reached the requisite stage in their development. Knowing *when* to make an uncovering intervention, then, is extremely important. This is to say that leaders need to be aware that a member and the group are less ready to tolerate some issues within, say, the sixth to seventh sessions than they might be in the ninth or tenth session.

Recall the case of Jeff. Through the 11th session, neither the co-leaders, the members, nor the group as a whole was prepared to address the fact that he covered his private parts with his hands whenever he talked about his concerns with dating women. Not until the co-leaders felt the group and they themselves were ready to face this issue did they call attention to Jeff's habit in a session. Because the leaders "dared" to demonstrate that they were willing to face this anxiety-laden topic—that is, go where the group as a whole was fearful of going—the group was provided with a solution that it could tolerate. The members in subsequent sessions were then able to address a multitude of issues evoked by the theme of sexuality.

History

Earlier we said that *history* refers to those member, leader, and group behaviors that have occurred since the inception of the group. Over the course of many sessions, a member may be observed to display certain habitual or patterned behaviors in response to certain emotion-laden issues or to certain behaviors of other members, the leaders, or the group as a whole. Employing these familiar and safe (but not enabling) solutions may be blocking the member's growth.

Frequently such behaviors are so much a part of a regular response pattern, that the member is unaware of engaging in them. By observing each member's patterns of behavior, leaders not only gain much knowledge about the individual members but also acquire an excellent vehicle for making a leader-to-member intervention. Perhaps such an intervention will reveal to the member for the first time the fact that he or she employs a certain restrictive solution every time a certain emotionally charged event occurs. Calling upon a historically patterned set of behaviors makes the intervention that more powerful.

To illustrate, suppose a therapist says the following: "Frank, I have observed you now for the past five sessions. Each time you've had an interaction with Sandra, your voice tone has become softer and you have repeated your statements. However, when you interact with Mike, your voice tone is elevated and your statements are clear and direct. What do you attribute this difference to?" By observing Frank's behavior over several sessions (as opposed to a first-time singular observation), the leader was able to reveal to Frank his behavior pattern. Now this pattern will no longer be part of Frank's subconscious. Now that he has been confronted with it, he will have the opportunity to face his disturbing motive(s), which may lead him to employ more enabling solutions in the future.

For the group as a whole, history is an accumulation of issues, behaviors, and affect, along with the patterned responses the group engages in in an attempt to manage anxiety-provoking events. When leaders link content and affect from session to session, each session is seen as part of a continuum of occurrences rather than as a discrete event. By making a group-as-a-whole observation of these patterned responses, leaders enable the group to move from the place where it is stuck. To illustrate how such an intervention can be made, we use an example from a group one of us was co-leading. Shortly after the group's third session began, I noted to myself that it had once again successfully managed to avoid facing an issue related to emotional intimacy. Rather than allowing this to go by, I chose to bring it up directly: I intervened with an observation meant to inform the group as a whole of its tendency to sidestep this particular matter. I said that perhaps the issue was still too difficult to face head-on, but because this was the third session in which it had come up, it was probably too important to ignore any longer. I suggested that the group might want to consider what it was about the topic that made it one to be avoided. The intervention made visible for the group as a whole the fact that it was faced with a disturbing motive and its pattern of behavior was clearly not resolving it. The solution was made obvious: It is okay to talk about what makes this topic toxic. This made it much safer to address the topic during this early stage of the group's life.

Stage Appropriate

Throughout this book, we have regularly referred to the need for leaders to be sensitive to what stage the group is in and to implement interventions that take this stage of development into account. Here we discuss how to implement stage-appropriate interventions in more detail.

The considerations that prompt stage-appropriate interventions are akin to those parents need to take into account when intervening with their children. Obviously the types of interventions that parents make during the first years of their child's life are quite different from those they make when the child is an adolescent or a young adult. The function and purpose of a parental intervention are largely determined by the developmental stage the child has reached—and the needs that are consistent with that stage. So, too, therapists need to take into account the stage at which the group has arrived and to use only interventions that address the developmental needs of the group at that stage.

In the first stage of the group's life, the leaders' primary focus is on creating norms and building a group culture that will make it safe for members to take risks and to grow. As the group's need for safety is met and it continues to develop, each subsequent stage will require that leaders be sensitive to its needs and the needs of its individual members.

Interpretation

The wife of one of us, who is an elementary school teacher, has a saying that helps her decide when and how to intervene in the classroom: "I'd rather be the guide on the side than the sage on the stage." This saying seems to us appropriate for group therapists when they are considering whether to make an interpretive intervention, for its thrust reminds leaders of their need to shrink their position in the group and to increase the positions of the members. Further, it implies the need for leaders to realize they are there to facilitate the release of the collective wisdom of the group. This primary task can only be achieved if leaders encourage members to provide feedback to one another (consensual validation) and confront and help members to interpret the motives underlying their behaviors. As members become more adept at making process interpretations, the power of the group becomes greater. But what of the leaders? What is their role in helping members achieve this skill? Once members have achieved it, what remains for the leaders to do?

Throughout this part on interventions, we have stressed that group therapists must heed group process and ensure that their interventions are process oriented. There is a difference between saying "I have just observed the way you interacted with Irene. Your jaw was set, your voice tone was intense, and you were sitting back in your chair" and "I think you have an issue with women who assert themselves." The former addresses the *way* the member presented himself. His behaviors were sketched so that he could see them. The tone and content of the intervention were designed to make it less likely that the member would erect defenses and more likely that he would become aware of *how* he behaved with Irene. Such an intervention is especially appropriate in the earlier stages of the group's life, when members and the group as a whole are not able to tolerate a more emotionally intrusive interpretation.

The second intervention is emotionally intrusive, so the member would be more inclined to take up a defensive posture—particularly if such an intervention were offered early in the group's life, before a safe climate wherein such observations could be tolerated had been established. Even later in the group's life, leaders need to be sensitive to the needs of the individual member and the group as a whole and consider their preparedness before making such an intervention.

What we are saying here is that interpretive interventions should follow a developmental sequence. Building upon *historical** data gained from session to session, leaders can help members to become progressively more self-aware and introspective. This teaches them to become more self-reliant when confronted with an interpretive intervention.

By turning to group members and asking them to comment on a transaction they have just observed between member and member, member and leader, or member and group, leaders encourage members to become process sensitive. At such times, leaders can offer corrective feedback on observations made by members that seem to be inaccurate, thus facilitating the learning process that has as its ultimate objective getting members to rely more on themselves and one another than on the leader for such commentary. For example, student co-leaders in one of our courses were repeatedly challenged by one member about their preparedness to lead

---

*We point out here that one session can constitute a *brief* history of member and/or group behaviors. Thus when a member is seen to repeat a certain behavior within a session, the leader or members may comment on it.

the group. Kevin, one of the co-leaders, finally responded, "You know, Bryan, this is not the first time you've questioned our qualifications for leading this group. Clearly this is a concern of yours. I am not sure what that is all about. I wonder if we can turn to the rest of the group and ask them what they have seen happening and to share how they feel about it. Maybe by seeking their input, it will help us figure out what's happening here."

Let us examine the various levels of this intervention. Note that the co-leader's interpretation was limited to the *process* of Bryan's comments. At the same time, the leader shrank his central position by stating that he did not know Bryan's hidden motives (that is, Kevin avoided psychologizing Bryan). This minimized Bryan's need to be defensive. By turning to the group, Kevin not only was encouraging them to offer process commentary but was also placing himself in a position to be more objective and thus able to offer corrective process commentary.* In this way, Kevin set the model for future sessions, in which the co-leaders would gradually reduce their central position as the group advanced to the later stages, freeing them to assume the roles of expert and authority on process to whom the members might defer.

Confrontation

One of us (Donigian, 1993) has written an article on the act of confrontation in which he referred to it as the art or skill of identifying and illuminating the incongruent behavior in which an individual member or the group as a whole is engaged. Confrontation is an act of grace in which the confronter is showing that he or she cares enough about the

---

*He also did what is called "going one down." To see what this means, imagine that in a conflicted situation you refuse to climb up the ladder, over your antagonist, but instead elect to climb one rung down. The effect of Kevin's "going one down" here was to diffuse the situation in order to deal with it more rationally.

relationship with the other to risk experiencing the discomfort of controversy in order to move that relationship toward greater emotional and psychological intimacy.

Confrontation is as concerned with process as are any of the other interventions we have discussed so far. As leaders, we need to be consciously aware that leader-to-member, leader-to-group, member-to-member, member-to-group, and group-to-member confrontations will occur, sooner or later, as a natural part of the group's development. When people hear the word *confrontation*, they usually envision individuals firing away at each other in a destructive, noncaring way. This should *not* be the practice in group. Leaders have the responsibility to demonstrate the art and skill of confrontation and to reframe it as an act of grace and caring, so that members will see this intervention as a means for achieving greater intimacy.

Another way of viewing confrontation is to see it as a form of feedback, one in which the focus is on the incongruence between a person's intentions and his or her behaviors (or those of the group). The confronter should also convey how the person's incongruent behaviors have affected him or her.

In a certain short-term outpatient group, one of the members disclosed how much she had learned about herself thus far in group, and disclosed that the most significant thing she had learned was how to make certain that her words matched her feelings. She concluded by saying how excited she felt about sharing this awareness with the group. Throughout this disclosure, however, the member seemed anything but excited or enthused. In fact, her voice was quite devoid of feeling, her posture rigid and without animation.

The leader made the following objective observation in a gentle tone of voice: "Kate, you say you feel you've learned so much about yourself and that most importantly you've learned that in order to have more meaningful relationships you must match your words and behaviors to your feelings. You have even claimed that you're excited about this new knowledge. Yet, just now, I didn't hear any enthusiasm in your voice. Your posture was quite fixed, and I didn't see any physical gestures that were consistent with your stated feelings. This makes me doubt that you have really achieved the insight you've said you've achieved. I felt I had to give this observation to you because I'm concerned." What followed was a group discussion on how the confrontation was experienced by each of the members, including Kate.

This was a daring act on the part of the leader, for the intervention challenged the member's beliefs about herself and brought to light the incongruence between her statement and her behavior. Even though intervening in a caring and concerned manner, the leader was taking the risk that not only Kate, but the other group members as well, might feel threatened by the confrontation. However, by following the confrontation with a group discussion of the process the members had just witnessed, the leader was teaching the group *how* and *why* a confrontational act can be used in a caring way. Moreover, the discussion encouraged the revelation of disturbing motives the members held regarding the act of confrontation. Thus the group was able to see confrontation as an enabling solution.

Parallels Outside the Group

The ultimate goal of group therapy is to help members apply what they have learned inside the group to their outside-the-group experiences. One of the ways leaders help the group to achieve this goal is by encouraging members to draw parallels between their therapy group experience and their experience in other social groups.

Parallel interventions should be restricted to the later stages of the group (work and termination). Members will surely attempt to bring the "outside" into the "inside" of the group during the early stages, but they will not have the necessary self-knowledge and ability to transfer self-corrective behaviors learned within the group to the outside until the later stages of therapy. In the early stages, members rely on old and familiar behaviors and apply inaccurate self-perceptions both inside and outside the group. Only when they have faced conflict while maintaining their newly acquired self-perceptions and interpersonal skills in group and learned that they have a *choice* of responses are they ready to make a full transition to their other worlds.

Once again, we remind you that the group is a microcosm of the world in which members function. Consequently, leaders can facilitate members' successful transition to that world by encouraging them to share their outside experiences with the group and giving them opportunities to see how their behavior inside the group parallels their behavior outside it. One of the ways leaders can do this is to use a subgroup for validation. If a leader knows that a member arrives and leaves group regularly with certain other members, and probably socializes with them at other times, the leader can solicit a form of consensual validation by asking those with whom the member subgroups whether the member's behaviors within the group are consistent with his or her behaviors outside it.

Sequencing

Sequencing of interventions is perhaps the most subtly effective intervention available to group leaders. Though it is frequently the least used intervention by new group therapists, sequencing is a much-discussed and continually evolving intervention among group therapists who remain students of group therapy (Dies, 1994; Yalom, 1985). It is generally thought of as one of the most artful parts of therapy (Yalom, 1985).

Sequencing of interventions requires group therapists to develop a fine sense of timing and an acute ability to recognize a member's and/or the group's readiness for more intimate and interpretive interventions. It also requires leaders to consider the stage appropriateness of their interventions and to acquire the abilities to use group history, to employ terms that reflect the feeling states of members and the group, to reframe process and content in ways that help members and the group see them in a new light, and, last but not least, to anticipate how an intervention will lead a member to change. Actually, these are but a few of the considerations experienced group therapists process before they implement an intervention! *How* a leader brings all of these considerations together into a Gestalt-like whole and turns them into a sequence of interventions is an art.

Most therapists need quite a bit of experience leading groups before they develop the sixth sense that enables them to sequence interventions effectively. However, certain elements in the sequencing process are fairly constant and thus can be learned quickly by beginner therapists. The stage appropriateness of an intervention is one of these elements.

Early in the second session of a group, one of the members for the third time questioned a statement I had made. I was sensitive to the process that was occurring between us. However, rather than offer an *interpretation* of his behavior—which I thought it was too soon to do—I said that this was the third question he had asked of me, and that after answering the first two, I realized that he already seemed to know the answers to his questions. Therefore, I said, perhaps he might try to reframe such questions as statements. By addressing the content and process of the transaction, I did not put the member on the defensive; instead, I enabled him to respond to my intervention.

Several weeks later, I observed to this member that when he spoke up in group, he continually turned to look at me, and that he also had the habit of prefacing his remarks by referring to his experience as a plant manager or to an author whose work he had read recently. I then remarked that he seemed to be trying to be part of the group and that it looked to me as if he wanted to get close to the others. However, I noted, his regular references to his managerial position and to experts whom he had read had the effect of placing himself above the rest of the members, and even of distancing himself from me. Before I spoke, I had taken into careful consideration the stage the group was in and the member's readiness to receive feedback on the effect his behavior was having upon the group as a whole and upon me. I also offered the observation that his taking the initiative in group conveyed his intention to be included and become close to the members. This subtle interpretation of his behavior was allowable, I felt, for he had been regularly taking the initiative over several sessions.

Two weeks later, the member was still behaving in the same manner. I then said that he had claimed at the start to be unable to establish intimate relationships (this was why he was in therapy), and that as I had observed him over time, I had seen him separating himself from the group. I observed that the members only *seemed* to accommodate him now whenever he spoke. I added that he appeared to be isolated in the group, and that if this was true, was this what he meant by his disclosure that he was unable to experience intimacy in his outside-group relationships? He admitted that this was the case. I responded that he had been given feedback for several weeks now on how his behavior was affecting others and how it had led to his isolation, and yet he seemed to be ignoring this message. I concluded that in all likelihood he was behaving similarly in other parts of his life, and that he was now in a position to decide whether he wanted to continue in the same way or to change.

This intervention seemed appropriate. It was sensitive to the developmental stage the group had reached, it pointed out to the member how the group as a whole was responding to him, it referred to his historical patterns of behavior, and it reflected feeling words such as *lonely*, *isolated*, and *intimacy*. We trust you can see why this intervention would have been out of place in the third or fourth session. At that point, the member would not have been ready for change.

Theme Identification and Interpretation

In Part III, we presented *themes* as one of the factors that influences member, leader, and group behavior. Before you read this section, we encourage you to refamiliarize yourself with that part of the book if it is not still fresh in your mind.

Here we reframe *themes* slightly to say that interpreting and identifying them is an intervention that can produce a profound influence on members and the group as a whole. When we discussed themes as a factor in Part III, we stressed that their identification can lead to releasing covert issues, noting how conscious and subconscious motives on the part of members, leaders, and the group as a whole can be brought to the surface. There we also said that themes provide leaders with a means for linking one session to another. It is to this dimension of themes that we return here.

Linking one session to the next unifies the group. Thus leaders who learn to attend to themes have the means for helping the group move forward. This will be noticeable in the depth of members' involvement with covert issues and the extent to which they explore their unconscious or disturbing motives. Linking themes shows individual members that an issue is not singularly theirs; when interpreted more broadly, the issue can involve every other member. The effect is that every member has the opportunity to work through his or her related issue. The consequence of such work is a deeper emotional bond among members.

Recall our earlier account of the member who revealed to the group her feelings about the recent funeral of her grandmother. The leaders were able to use her self-disclosure to reframe death as a universal theme the whole group could relate to. Consequently, each member was given permission to address his or her related issue in the following sessions. Had the co-leaders failed to universalize the theme, the group probably would have continued to faltered uncomfortably in the presence of the woman's grief until another unrelated issue was raised. Frequently, this is what happens in group—members go from one unrelated issue to the next, without fully dealing with any of them. We refer to this phenomenon as "setting a lot of little fires," none of which get attended to and all of which eventually die out. Therapy groups that do this take on the aspect of public forums where different issues are aired from session to session. The content of each issue belongs to the presenter; there is often little or no personal meaning to the issue for the other members. Under these circumstances, the group invests little in any of the issues presented, and misses the opportunity to grow by exploring any issue in depth.

BLOCKS TO EFFECTIVE INTERVENTIONS

Now that we have considered some of the interventions available to leaders, we turn to some of the barriers that prevent leaders from making effective interventions.

Anxiety

Recall that we said earlier that anxiety is a state of continual tension resulting from unsuccessful attempts to cope with internal conflicts, the roots of which lie in earlier conflicts that took place in our first group—our family of origin. Also recall that we noted all three elements—leader(s), members, and the group itself—must learn to tolerate increasing levels of anxiety in order to do effective therapeutic work. Too frequently, leaders' own low tolerance for anxiety drives them to enlist restrictive solutions. We have observed our own trainees become so overwhelmed by an intense self-disclosure by a member that they fail to intervene when the group responds by fleeing from the intensity of the moment. The result is that group tension intensifies until a solution is introduced that will reduce the tension. Such solutions are usually restrictive. They supply a temporary fix, but the group loses an important opportunity to grow.

New Group Leaders' Fears and Fantasies

"How do you remember all this?" "There is just too much to remember; I am afraid I won't remember it all." "I was afraid to say anything because I might miss something else!" "I was afraid the group (or the member) might fall apart and I would not be able to stitch it (or the member) back together." "What happens if a member really gets angry and tries to physically attack another member?"

This is just a small sampling of the type of responses a random number of group leaders gave to the question: "What were the most anxious moments you have faced as a group leader?" Though the results of this survey of over 400 group leaders are still being analyzed, our preliminary conclusion is that new group leaders often feel insecure because they do not truly understand the group process. Their tendency is to focus more on content—that is, on what is being said—than on process—on how it is being said.

New leaders are frequently at a loss concerning how to establish group norms and standards. They are afraid to stay with and trust what they feel most comfortable with at this point in their development, even though in all likelihood the group will not press them to go beyond that boundary. New leaders also seem to avoid the risk of pushing beyond their own parameters of safety because they fear if they do so, some catastrophic event will befall the group. There is always the chance that such an event may occur, but the process is resilient, and so (generally) are the members. Almost certainly (and we speak with 25 years of experience behind us) the members, the group, and the leaders themselves will recover from the event. Still, it is hard to convince inexperienced group leaders to push those boundaries. Most prefer to deflect the tension by employing restrictive solutions. They then find themselves faced with another one of their dreads—the group is not progressing.

Lack of Follow-Through

Those of you who have engaged in any form of athletic activity are familiar with this concept. Among the most often cited reasons for an unsuccessful athletic attempt—whether it be shooting a basket, fly fishing, throwing a baseball, bowling, or making a golf shot—is lack of follow-through. For the same reason, very many leader interventions are unsuccessful. Most new leaders fail to visualize the sequencing of the intervention process. Frequently, they make an intervention, the member or the group responds, and that is where they allow the transaction to end. The leader fails to follow through with another intervention that will move the response to a more intrapersonal or interpersonal level.

An example of the value of follow-through occurred with Jeff. Once the co-leaders felt comfortable enough to raise the issue that he covered his private parts when speaking of dating women and Jeff acknowledged doing so, the leaders followed through by encouraging him to talk about it. More importantly, they universalized the issue, which led to interpersonal interactions among the other group members. Had the leaders not followed through in these ways, a good opportunity for Jeff and the others to learn more about themselves would have passed.

Lack of Clear Goals

It has long been our position that one of the most neglected matters in group therapy is the need to set clear goals. When members, leaders, and the group as a whole do not understand why they are coming together, the group functions in a rather haphazard fashion, like a ship without a rudder. It is generally up to the leaders to establish the group's goals and to help each member state what she or he hopes to learn or change as a result of being in the group.

Failure to set clear goals considerably reduces the types of interventions available to the group leaders. How can the leaders confront the group as a whole or its members about incongruent behaviors if the desired changes were not clearly articulated when the group formed? Leaders are then prevented from mentioning the unmentionable, from drawing parallels to members' experiences outside the group, from making sequential interventions that challenge the members' desire to change.

Critics of goal-setting contend that it risks making the group, the members, and the leaders microfocused. They remind us that the whole purpose of joining a group is to gain insights into oneself through the interpersonal, interactional nature of the group process, and that that purpose will be lost if all three elements concentrate exclusively on specific behavior change. We do not disagree with this criticism. However, we counter it by insisting that the leaders of interactive groups are responsible for setting goals for the group and the members that are both broad enough to avoid this pitfall and personal enough so that all members will take ownership of their reasons for being in the group.

Lack of Norms

Actually, there is no such thing as a group without norms, either implied or explicit. Every person who joins the group brings into it his or her preexisting set of norms. The same can be said for the leaders. Moreover, as a group develops, it evolves its own collective set of norms. How, then, can we say treat "lack of norms" as a block to effective intervention? What we mean here by *lack of norms* is that leaders have not established norms in the early stages of the group that will tolerate increasing levels of acceptable behaviors by members and the group as a whole. The result is that the safety experienced by the members is reduced, their willingness to risk new behaviors is minimized, and the tendency to conform is increased. If *what* can be talked about and *how* it can be talked about are restricted during the course of the group's development, it follows that the number and kinds of leader interventions that will be available and tolerated will also be limited. In contrast, if leaders help members and the group as a whole widen their boundaries of acceptable behaviors, the members and the group as whole will be able to tolerate the types of interventions that encourage increasing self-exploration and interpersonal interaction.

Recall the group in which Harry, in the first session, announced his concerns about his bisexuality. The individual members and the group as a whole showed little tolerance for him. Had we not addressed the members' and the group's response immediately, had we instead simply allowed them to stand, we would have been in complicity with them. In effect, we would have helped establish a norm that restricted *how* and *what* could be safely talked about. Then, in subsequent sessions of that group, we would have found ourselves restricted in the types of interventions we could make (such as sequencing, confrontation, theme building, self-disclosure, and mentioning the unmentionable).

We must repeat again, because this is such an important point, that the extent to which the group as a whole and its members will develop increasing levels of accommodating norms directly depends on what the leaders can tolerate themselves.

Doing Individual Therapy

It should be obvious that when leaders conduct individual therapy within the group, they are weakening or destroying the interactive nature of group process. We question the reason for forming a group in the first place if the leaders do not intend to take advantage of the power that resides within the group as a whole, instead preferring to conduct individual therapy in a group format. Clearly the interventions available to such leaders will be limited to those that allow for just that—doing individual therapy. Consequently, nearly all of the interventions we presented earlier would be out of bounds for them.

Premature Termination

Premature termination refers to a gamut of early endings by members and their reasons for leaving (Bernard, 1994; Lothstein, 1993; Yalom, 1985). Our focus here, however, is on how the premature ending of the group as a whole can block effective interventions.

When we addressed the termination stage of the group in Part III, we said that often this was the stage that received the least attention from group leaders, though it is equal in importance to the first four stages. Generally, groups that terminate prematurely are those that never developed beyond the first two stages of group life for any of several reasons: inadequate selection and preparation of members, restrictive norms and standards that led to a culture that minimized safety and refused to tolerate risky behavior, or leaders' own low tolerance for ever-widening levels of acceptable group and member behaviors. In such a group, there are no opportunities for implementing sequential interventions, interpretation, mentioning the unmentionable, use of group history, drawing on parallels from outside of the group, conscious and subconscious issues, and the tolerance for confrontation.

Once the group does develop beyond the third stage, it is important for leaders not to mistake the work stage (Stage 4) for the termination stage (Stage 5). This is especially the case with time-limited groups, where there is a preset number of sessions. Leaders need to work hard to keep the group from bolting too early. If they don't, they will have lost the opportunity to help members learn how to make a successful transition from the group to their other social environments. They will have neglected to make the interventions that would allow members to share how they are applying the knowledge they acquired in group and the changes they made there to their external social groups. They will also have failed to make the kind of interventions that would help members deal effectively with the theme(s) still present as the group disbands.

Resistance? Difficult Group? Member? Or What?

"The group's silence was really tough tonight." "What is it with Joe? He really has been taking up a lot of the group's time lately." "Did you watch that? All she did was reject the help that was being offered her, while continuing to say how impatient she feels because nothing she does seems to work." "Every time Susan tried to get off the hot seat, the group seemed to find a way to push her back on it." "What is it with me? This is the third session in a row in which the group got on my case for not being a helpful therapist." "Frank keeps telling Marie how she reminds him of his mother, and she continues to take care of him." "What about David threatening to leave the group again? Only tonight the group did not try and stop him."

These comments, familiar to anyone who has ever led a therapy group, are just a sample of the myriad forms resistance can take. For some therapists, resistance is a block to the therapeutic process; for others, it is an opportunity to move the therapeutic process forward.

How is it that resistance can be perceived as positive by some and negative by others? No other term in the language of psychotherapy generates such bipolar views as *resistance*. Small wonder, then, that how a therapist views the process of resistance will determine how he or she will manage this phenomenon. Therapists who take the position that resistance is countertherapeutic will use interventions that in all likelihood will perpetuate it rather than relieve it. In contrast, therapists who view resistance as natural, even necessary to the advancement of the therapeutic process at times, will when it arises employ interventions that facilitate the therapeutic process.

One group was midway into its third session when a member challenged the qualifications of one of our student leaders. The leader viewed this as a personal challenge and responded by saying, "I fail to see how answering your question will help the group or yourself, for it seems to me that you have a problem with authority." The member's reaction was to withdraw from the group. Whereupon two other members turned to the leader and stated that her response was a good example of why they, too, questioned her qualifications. Within moments, the entire group was challenging the therapist.

Had this leader understood the first member's question as a natural and clear sign that the issues of trust and security were being raised, her reply might have sounded something like this: "I'll be glad to answer your question. However, it will help me if you would tell me how my answer will help you. I would like to be as specific as I can." Not only does this response consider the member's (and group's) need to establish safety and trust, it also addresses the metacommunication of the member and the group's stage of development. Contrasted with the first response, it acknowledges that the member's question was natural and to be expected— thus advancing the therapeutic process.

There is substantial support for taking this kind of stance toward resistance. Yalom (1985), for example, argues that "Resistance is not an impediment to therapy but is the stuff of therapy" (p. 451). MacKenzie (1994) says that "Resistance is . . . an indication that the group is in the right area" (p. 53), while Porter (1994) believes that "Resistance is a normal reaction to growth [and it] is needed for self-protection and healing" (p. 104).

Resistance is usually activated when a system's homeostasis is being challenged. In psychotherapy groups, the members, leaders, and the group itself are all being challenged to change and/or grow. Change and/or growth cannot happen without some level of conflict (that is, a threat to the system), which naturally creates some anxiety. Referring back to Whitaker and Lieberman's focal conflict model, we can frame resistance as the employment of restrictive solutions in order to lessen the effect of anxiety. These restrictive solutions take a variety of forms, such as monopolizing, scapegoating, arriving late, skipping sessions, subgrouping, mass group denial, premature termination, challenging the therapist, collusion of the therapists with the group to eliminate a member, transference, countertransference, rejecting help, and silence. If therapists understand that all of these are manifestations of anxiety and are associated with a real or imagined fear (reactive motive), they will take heart when they occur for they will know that the therapeutic process is working. They will realize that their task is to encourage the member, the group, or even themselves to feel safe and to disclose the disturbing motive.

For example, whenever he was asked to share his thoughts and feelings, Jason had a patterned response: he avoided answering with a statement; instead, he answered with a question. The effect was to emotionally distance himself from the other members. This form of withdrawal had continued through a number of sessions, until finally Jason was no longer being addressed by the other members. One of the risks for the leader at a moment like this is to look for a quick fix. Obviously a great deal was going on with all three elements in this situation. At the member level, Jason's response was communicating his feelings of insecurity. Perhaps his disturbing motive was a desire to be included in the group, but he feared that disclosing anything about himself would lead to the group's nonacceptance of him (reactive motive). He chose instead to engage in a restrictive solution that he was familiar with and that made him feel secure. As, one by one, the members who had tried to connect with him discontinued their efforts, Jason found the distance between himself and the rest of the group widening. All of the other members had originally voiced their disturbing motives through their desire to draw him in (enabling solution), only to be met with his restrictive solution. This gradually led to the development of a reactive motive in each of the other members, which probably went something like this: "He isn't worth the trouble. He only will pull back further anyway." In turn, this led to the individual members' restrictive solutions of ignoring him to the point of denying his presence. Eventually the group as a whole engaged in the restrictive solution of totally excluding Jason.

What about the leader element at this juncture? The fact that the situation had gotten this far suggests that the leader may have been applying his or her own restrictive solution(s) to the events as they unfolded. A leader's desire to avoid appearing inept (disturbing motive) for fear of being discounted by the group (reactive motive) easily evolves into the employment of a restrictive solution—as was done here when Jason's group leader allowed events to escalate to such a point. (Other forms of leader restrictive solutions might include blaming Jason for not making a statement and chastising the group for ganging up on him.) These types of solutions result from a leader's resistance to acknowledging disturbing incidents.

What would have happened if the leader had decided to nip the incident in the bud? Had the leader done this by employing any of the following interventions, events might have taken an entirely different course.

Suppose the leader chose to intervene at the member-to-member level the moment Jason's patterned response was observed. This might have encouraged a continuation of the interaction between Jason and the first member who reached out to him. The leader could have accomplished this intervention by asking both of them to talk through what each of them had experienced, and to explore the feelings that had been generated by the experience. This member-to-member intervention would have placed the resolution of the conflict in the hands of the two principal players in the transaction.

The leader would not have ignored the effect these two members' interaction was having on the other members and the group as a whole. In fact, after Jason and the first member completed their dialoguing, the leader could have employed a group-as-a-whole intervention by asking the group how it had been affected by the interaction between Jason and the other member. This kind of group-to-member intervention would draw upon the power of the group—through the use of feedback, consensual validation, and so on concerning the effect these two members' behaviors had had upon the others.

In addition, a brief group-as-a-whole process illumination could have prevented the group and Jason from continuing down the path of group denial (flight) and individual member (Jason) withdrawal. Such an intervention might have taken the following form: "It seems that you [the group] have been neglecting to include Jason in much of your interactions recently. If it would be of any help, I noticed it appeared to happen after a number of you tried to bring him in but were met, instead, by Jason's questioning of you. I wonder if any of you would care to comment on that." Notice that the leader does not scold either the group or Jason. Instead, the intervention simply makes note of the *way* (process) things have unfolded in the group and conveys to the group that is has the ability to deal with the incident. Once again, the intervention is designed to release the power of the group to address how it is using its restrictive solution, while giving Jason the opportunity to address his disturbing motive for employing his restrictive solution.

When we contrast what happened with what might have happened in this group, we realize how important it is for leaders to be well aware of themselves. This means knowing one's strengths, limitations, and vulnerabilities. We cannot sufficiently underscore the need for therapists to pursue self-knowledge continually. Questioning what it is about ourselves that led us to respond in a certain way to a member, the group, or an event fosters our self-understanding. What's more, such questioning can be self-empowering. For example, you might ask yourself why you saw a certain moment in group as resistance, while your co-leader viewed the same moment as a stimulus to self-reflection. When we consider the two different approaches to managing Jason and the group he was in, we realize that the (theoretical) leader who opted to use any or all of the interventions we illustrated might have had a strong sense of him- or herself and there-fore be less threatened by what occurred than the other (real-life) leader was. The ability to use resistance to move a member, the group, and perhaps oneself to a more effective way of addressing conflict is a great talent in a group leader.

Whatever form resistance takes, the group therapist needs to keep foremost in mind that the power for change rests with the group. Thus it is essential that the means for dealing with resistance be found in the group itself. Enlisting the assistance of group members to deal with resistance makes the task less difficult for the therapist (Spotnitz, 1952). We have also seen the group, without any prompting from us, confront the resistance of an individual member, the leader(s), and even of itself (for example: "We seem to be spinning our wheels. What are we avoiding?").

The management of resistance in all of its forms may be addressed through any of a number of interventions, including member-to-member, group-to-member, group-as-a-whole, and brief (but not interpretive) process observations that solicit further observations and interpretations from members and/or the group. It is important to remember that resistance is an opportunity to move a member, the group, or even yourself to a more effective way of addressing a particular conflict.

Agazarian and Janoff (1993) are of the opinion that "Members in systems-centered groups [should be] encouraged to understand how defenses relate to the management of frustration with the goal of tolerating frustration as a natural process, for neither the self, the situation, nor another is to blame" (p. 39). Their message is clear: leaders must continually be aware that the resolution to resistance has to go through the group as a whole and/or its members.

So what do the phrases *difficult member* and *tough group* mean? For us (Donigian & Malnati, 1987), they signify opportunities to move the member(s) and/or the group forward. We refuse to view them as a *negative* valence that will *block* us from making effective interventions. We hope you agree.

Epilogue

We hope you have found this journey through the demysti-fication of group process enlightening. As you continue to reframe group process as the systemic interaction of the three primary elements, we trust that through practice you will *master* it and you will find it is all the technique you will ever need.

BIBLIOGRAPHY

Agazarian, Y. M., & Peters, R. (1981). *The visible and invisible group: Two perspectives on group psychotherapy and group process*. London: Rutledge & Kegan Paul.

Agazarian, Y. M., & Janoff, S. (1993). A systems theory and small groups. In H. I. Kaplan & B. J. Saddock (Eds.), *Comprehensive group psychotherapy* (3rd ed.). Baltimore: Williams & Wilkins.

Bernard, H. S. (1994). Difficult patients and challenging situations. In H. S. Bernard & K. R. MacKenzie (Eds.), *Basics of group psychotherapy*. New York: The Guilford Press.

Bernard, H. S., & MacKenzie, K. Roy (Eds.). (1994). *Basics of group psychotherapy*. New York: The Guilford Press.

Carroll, M., & Wiggins, J. (1990). *Elements of group counseling: Back to basics*. Denver: Love.

Corey, G. (1990). *Theory and practice of group counseling* (3rd ed.). Pacific Grove, CA: Brooks/Cole.

Davidson, M. (1983). *Uncommon sense: The life and thought of Ludwig von Bertalanffy*. Los Angeles: J. P. Archer.

Dies, R. R. (1994). The therapist's role in group treatments. In H. S. Bernard & K. Roy MacKenzie (Eds.), *Basics of group psychotherapy*. New York: The Guilford Press.

Donigian, J. (1993). Group reflections. *Together, 22*(1), 6.

Donigian, J., & Malnati, R. (1987). *Critical incidents in group therapy*. Pacific Grove, CA: Brooks/Cole.

Durkin, H. E. (1981). General system theory and group psychotherapy. In J. E. Durkin (Ed.), *Living groups: Group psychotherapy and general system theory*. New York: Brunner/Mazel.

Durkin, J. E. (Ed.). (1981). *Living groups: Group psychotherapy and general system theory*. New York: Brunner/Mazel.

Foulkes, S. H. (1964). *Therapeutic group analysis*. New York: International Universities Press.

Gladding, S. T. (1991). *Group work*. New York: Merrill.

Hansen, J. C., Warner, R. W., & Smith, E. J. (1980). *Group counseling: Theory and process* (2nd ed.). Boston: Allyn & Bacon.

Heider, J. (1985). *The tao of leadership*. New York: Bantam.

Horwitz, L. (1993). Group centered models of group psychotherapy. In H. I. Kaplan & B. J. Saddock (Eds.), *Comprehensive group psychotherapy* (3rd ed.). Baltimore: Williams & Wilkins.

Jacobs, E. E., Harvill, R. L., & Masson, R. L. (1994). *Group counseling strategies and skills* (2nd ed.). Pacific Grove, CA: Brooks/Cole.

Kaplan, H. I., & Saddock, B. J. (Eds.). (1993). *Comprehensive group psychotherapy* (3rd ed.). Baltimore: Williams & Wilkins.

Kottler, J. E. (1994). *Advanced group leadership*. Pacific Grove, CA: Brooks/Cole.

Levine, B. (1991). *Group psychotherapy*. Prospect Heights, IL: Waveland.

Lothstein, L. M. (1993). Termination process: Processes in group psychotherapy. In H. I. Kaplan & B. J. Saddock (Eds.), *Comprehensive group psychotherapy* (3rd ed.). Baltimore: Williams & Wilkins.

MacKenzie, K. Roy (1994). The developing structure of the therapy group system. In H. S. Bernard & K. Roy MacKenzie (Eds.), *Basics of group psychotherapy*. New York: The Guilford Press.

Munich, R. L. (1993). Group dynamics. In H. I. Kaplan & B. J. Saddock (Eds.), *Comprehensive group psychotherapy* (3rd ed.). Baltimore: Williams & Wilkins.

Napier, R. W., & Gershenfeld, M. K. (1993). *Group theory and practice* (5th ed.). Boston: Houghton Mifflin.

Nichols, M. P., & Schwartz, R. C. (1994). *Family therapy: Concepts and methods* (3rd ed.). Boston: Allyn & Bacon.

Piper, W. E., & McCallum, M. (1994). Selection of patients for group interventions. In H. S. Bernard & K. Roy MacKenzie (Eds.), *Basics of group psychotherapy*. New York: The Guilford Press.

Porter, K. (1994). Principles of group therapeutic technique. In H. S. Bernard & K. Roy MacKenzie (Eds.), *Basics of group psychotherapy*. New York: The Guilford Press.

Porter, K. (1993). Combined individual and group psychotherapy. In H. I. Kaplan & B. J. Saddock (Eds.), *Comprehensive group psychotherapy* (3rd ed.). Baltimore: Williams & Wilkins.

Roller, B., & Nelson, V. (1993). Cotherapy. In H. I. Kaplan & B. J. Saddock (Eds.), *Comprehensive group psychotherapy*. Baltimore: Williams & Wilkins.

Rutan, J. S., & Alonso, A. (1982). Group therapy, individual therapy, or both? *International Journal of Group Psychotherapy, 32,* 267.

Rutan, J. S., & Stone, W. N. (1984). *Psychodynamic group psychotherapy*. Lexington, KY: Collanmore.

Salvendy, J. T. (1993). Selection and preparation of patients and organization of the group. In H. I. Kaplan & B. J. Saddock (Eds.), *Comprehensive group psychotherapy* (3rd ed.). Baltimore: Williams & Wilkins.

Slavson, S. R. (1957). Are there group dynamics in therapy groups? *International Journal of Group Psychotherapy, 7,* 131–54.

Spotnitz, H. (1952). A psychoanalytic view of resistance in groups. *International Journal of Group Psychotherapy, 2,* 3.

Swogger, G., Jr. (1981). Human communication and group experience. In J. E. Durkin (Ed.), *Living groups: Group psychotherapy and general system theory*. New York: Brunner/Mazel.

Trotzer, J. P. (1977). *The counselor and the group*. Monterey, CA: Brooks/Cole.

Tuckman, B. W. (1965). Developmental sequence in small groups. *Psychological Bulletin, 63,* 384.

Vanderkolk, C. J. (1985). *Introduction to group counseling and psychotherapy*. Columbus, OH: Merrill.

Von Bertalanffy, L. (1968). *General systems theory: Foundations, development, application*. New York: Braziller.

Weiner, M. F. (1993). Role of the leader in group psychotherapy. In H. I. Kaplan & B. J. Saddock (Eds.), *Comprehensive group psychotherapy* (3rd ed.). Baltimore: Williams & Wilkins.

Whitaker, D. S., & Lieberman, M. (1964). *Psychotherapy through the group process*. New York: Atherton Press.

Yalom, I. D. (1985). *The theory and practice of group psychotherapy* (3rd ed.). New York: Basic Books.

INDEX

TO THE OWNER OF THIS BOOK:

We hope that you have found *Systemic Group Therapy: A Triadic Model* useful. So that this book can be improved in a future edition, would you take the time to complete this sheet and return it? Thank you.

School and address: _____

Department: _____

Instructor's name: _____

1. What I like most about this book is: _____

_____

_____

2. What I like least about this book is: _____

_____

_____

3. My general reaction to this book is: _____

_____

4. The name of the course in which I used this book is: _____

_____

5. Were all of the chapters of the book assigned for you to read?

If not, which ones weren't? _____

6. In the space below, or on a separate sheet of paper, please write specific suggestions for improving this book and anything else you'd care to share about your experience in using the book.

_____

_____

_____

Optional:

Your name: _____ Date: _____

May Brooks/Cole quote you, either in promotion for *Systemic Group Therapy: A Triadic Model* or in future publishing ventures?

Yes: _____ No: _____

Sincerely,

Jeremiah Donigian

FOLD HERE

- -

FOLD HERE